The Geography of
South Carolina

*Available from the Simms Initiatives and the
University of South Carolina Press*

The Army Correspondence of
Colonel John Laurens, ed.

As Good as a Comedy
and Paddy McGann

Beauchampe

Border Beagles

Carl Werner, 2 vols.

The Cassique of Kiawah

Castle Dismal

Charlemont

The Charleston Book, ed.

Confession

Count Julian

The Damsel of Darien, 2 vols.

Dramas: Norman Maurice, Michael
Bonham, and Benedict Arnold

Egeria

Eutaw

The Forayers

The Geography of South Carolina

The Golden Christmas

Guy Rivers

Helen Halsey

Historical and Political Poems (*which
includes* Monody, The Vision of Cortes,
The Tri-Color, Donna Florida, and
Charleston and Her Satirists)

The History of South Carolina

Joscelyn

Katharine Walton

The Letters of
William Gilmore Simms, Vol. 1

The Letters of
William Gilmore Simms, Vol. 2

The Letters of
William Gilmore Simms, Vol. 3

The Letters of
William Gilmore Simms, Vol. 4

The Letters of
William Gilmore Simms, Vol. 5

The Letters of
William Gilmore Simms, Vol. 6 (exp. ed.)

The Life of Captain John Smith

The Life of the Chevalier Bayard

The Life of Francis Marion

The Lily and the Totem

Marie de Berniere

Martin Faber and
Other Tales, 2 vols.

Mellichampe

The Partisan

Pelayo, 2 vols.

Poems, Descriptive, Dramatic,
Legendary, and Contemplative, 2 vols.

The Remains of
Maynard Davis Richardson

Richard Hurdis

Sack and Destruction of
the City of Columbia

The Scout

Selections from the
Letters and Speeches of the
Hon. James H. Hammond, ed.

Simms's Poems Areytos

Social and Political Prose:
Slavery in America/Father Abbot

South Carolina in the
Revolutionary War

Southward Ho!

Stories and Tales

A Supplement to the Plays
of William Shakespeare

Vasconselos

Views and Reviews in
American Literature,
History and Fiction, 2 vols.

Voltmeier

War Poetry of the South

The Wigwam and the Cabin

Woodcraft

The Yemassee

The Geography of
South Carolina

Being a Companion to the
History of that State

William Gilmore Simms

Critical Introduction by Sean R. Busick
With a Biographical Overview by David Moltke-Hansen

The University of South Carolina Press

New material © 2015 University of South Carolina

Cloth original published by Babcock & Co., 1843
Paperback published by the University of South Carolina Press
Columbia, South Carolina 29208

www.sc.edu/uscpress

Manufactured in the United States of America

24 23 22 21 20 19 18 17 16 15
10 9 8 7 6 5 4 3 2 1

ISBN 978-1-61117-478-6 (pbk)

Published in cooperation with the Simms Initiatives, a project of the University of South Carolina Libraries with the generous support of the Watson-Brown Foundation, and with additional funding by the John Govan Simms Endowment.

William Gilmore Simms: A Biographical Overview

David Moltke-Hansen

Introduction

Harper's Weekly put it succinctly in its July 2, 1870, issue: "In the death of Mr. Simms, on the 11th of June, at Charleston, the country has lost one more of its time-honored band of authors, and the South the most consistent and devoted of her literary sons" (qtd. In Butterworth and Kibler 125–26). Indeed no mid-nineteenth-century writer and editor did more than William Gilmore Simms to frame white southern self-identity and nationalism, shape southern historical consciousness, or foster the South's participation and recognition in the broader American literary culture. No southern writer enjoyed more contemporary esteem and attention, at least after Edgar Allan Poe moved north. Among American romancers (or writers of prose epics), only New Yorker James Fenimore Cooper was as successful by the 1840s. In those same years, Simms was the South's most influential editor of cultural journals. He also was the region's most prolific cultural journalist and poet, publishing an average of one book review and one poem per week for forty-five years.

Before his death Simms saw his national reputation fall along with the Confederacy he had vigorously supported and with the slave regime that many in the North had come to despise. Nevertheless reprints of most of the twenty titles in the selected edition of his works, first published between 1853 and 1860, appeared up until World War I. Thereafter only *The Yemassee*, an early romance about an Indian war in South Carolina, continued in print. The tide began to turn in the 1950s, when five volumes of Simms's letters appeared and a growing number of his works were issued in new editions. Publication in 1992 of the first literary biography, by John C. Guilds, and establishment of the William Gilmore Simms Society and the *Simms Review* the next year at once reflected and fostered this revived interest. Yet not until the 2011 launch of the digital Simms edition of the South Caroliniana Library of the University of South Carolina did scholars of southern, American, and nineteenth-century culture have the prospect of ready access to all of Simms's separately published works. With the University of South Carolina Press's cooperation, readers also will have access to sixty works in paperback editions by the end of 2014. Simms himself never saw nearly so many of his works in print at one time.

Clearly the decline in the critical standing of, and historical attention to, Simms and his oeuvre in the century after his death has reversed in the years since. The last three decades of the twentieth century saw more published on Simms than the previous hundred years (Butterworth and Kibler 126–200; MLA International). The last decade of the twentieth and first decade of the twenty-first centuries saw more dissertations and theses on him (forty-one) than had appeared in all the years before. This is not to say that Simms is yet given the attention directed to some of his contemporaries. For the first decade of the twenty-first century, the Modern Language Association International Bibliography lists roughly four times as many scholarly publications on James Fenimore Cooper, more than ten times as many on Nathaniel Hawthorne, and sixteen times as many on Edgar Allan Poe. Not surprisingly, therefore, Simms is not yet included in most anthologies of American literature, although he is a subject or a source in an expanding and ever more diverse body of scholarship.

To prepare to read Simms, it is important to see his writings in multiple contexts. He rarely wrote about himself outside of his more personal poems and his letters (some fifteen hundred of the many thousands of which survive). Yet he systematically drew on his background, personal experience, and relationships in his work. He also shaped that work through a progressively developed poetics and philosophy of life, history, and art. He did so in the context of his very broad reading of both contemporary and earlier Western literature and in the midst of multiple professional engagements and responsibilities. The richness and variety of these writings and involvements make Simms a key figure for future understanding of the literary culture, issues, and networks in mid-nineteenth-century America.

Background

Simms's family history reflected the dynamics that fueled the spread southward and westward of the populations, plantation economy, and society of the South Atlantic states. Simms's ancestry also reflected the Scots-Irish and English roots of what became identified as southern culture by the 1830s, a generation after the end of most immigration to the region. Two of Simms's grandparents, William and Elisabeth Sims, were Scots-Irish and migrated to South Carolina from Ulster. One, John Singleton, was an American-born son of putatively English immigrants, who had come to South Carolina from Virginia. The fourth, Jane Miller, was daughter of two Scots-Irish and Irish descended people—John Miller, of North and then South Carolina, and Jane Ross. Ross's family also migrated to South Carolina from western Virginia, where members lived cheek by jowl with other Scots-Irish families, who migrated to the Carolinas (White, *Ross*). Simms's father and Uncle James migrated in 1808 from Charleston to Tennessee, then to Mississippi. This was after the bankruptcy of the elder William's business and the deaths of his wife and their other two sons. Following the last of these losses, the elder Simms's hair turned white in a week. To his anguished eyes, Charleston appeared "a place of tombs" (qtd. in Guilds 6, 12).

For the son, however, Charleston was home—so much so that he refused to leave his maternal grandmother and move to Mississippi when his uncle came to get him in 1816. Then the fifth largest and by far the wealthiest city, as well as one of the greatest ports, in America, Charleston was at the peak of its influence (Moltke-Hansen, "Expansion" 25–31; Rogers). Cotton culture on the sea islands to the south, begun in 1790, and rice culture in impounded lowcountry tidal marshes meant that the port was filled not only with sailors of many lands and languages, but also with enslaved people of many African and Creole cultures and speech ways (slaves continued to be imported legally in large numbers until 1808). This street life made vivid the transnational nature of plantation agriculture and the fact that the developing region's dramatically expanding borders "were not just geographic; they also were human, historical, and intellectual" (Moltke-Hansen, "Southern" 19).

Even more important for the future author, the expanding region's borders and nature were taking imaginative shape. The West of the senior William Gilmore Simms and the first Creek War in which he fought, the Revolutionary War of the young Simms's maternal grandfather, the backcountry of many related Scots-Irish settlers, all these became grist for a lonely, energetic boy, who spent as much time with books as he could (Simms, *Letters* 1:161). The possibilities of such settings, incidents, and characters were not confined to history alone. Simms reported that he "used to glow and shiver in turn over 'The Pilgrim's Progress,'" while "Moses' adventures in 'The Vicar of Wakefield' threw [him] into paroxysms of laughter" (Hayne 261–62). Sir Walter Scott's Border and medieval romances and James Fenimore Cooper's Leatherstocking tales also deeply colored his imagination (Simms, *Views* 1:248, and Moltke-Hansen, "Southern" 6–15). As affecting were the ghost stories and Revolutionary War tales of his grandmother and the verses sent, and tales told, by his father.

These diverse tales became reasons to explore—in books, but also on the ground. As a boy, Simms ranged through the city and along the banks of the Ashley River, which fed into Charleston Harbor. He did so in search of scenes of colonial and Revolutionary battles and incidents (*Letters* 1:lxii). He first heard his uncle's and father's many Irish and frontier stories when they visited in Charleston in 1816 and 1818, respectively. He heard more on his trips to Mississippi during the winter of 1824 through the spring of 1825 and again in 1826. The first trip took him through Georgia and Alabama, where he saw elements of the Creek and Cherokee nations. At the time, Simms later reported, he was a boy "cumbered with fragmentary materials of thought, . . . choked by the tangled vines of erroneous speculation, and haunted by passions, which, like so many wolves, lurked, in ready waiting, for their unsuspecting prey" (*Social* 6). When he first got to Mississippi, traveling partly by stage, partly by riverboat, and partly by horse, Simms learned that his father had just come back from "a trip of three hundred miles into the heart of the Indian country" (Trent 15). Later father and son "rode together on horseback to various settlements on the frontier of Alabama and Mississippi" (Guilds 10–11, 17–18). Simms recalled as well "having traveled 150 miles beyond the Mississippi" (Shillingsburg, "Literary Grist" 120). The next year he returned to the Southwest by ship. "During this [second] trip he carried a 'note book.'" There he jotted episodes, encounters, stories heard, characters seen, and descriptions of the landscapes unfolding around him. He also wrote "at least sixteen poems" (Kibler, "First"; Shillingsburg, "Literary Grist" 123).

Simms took a third western trip five years later, writing letters back to the newspaper that by then he was editing (*Letters* 1:10–38). Together these three trips provided materials for his writings over more than forty years. "The first . . . produced mainly short fiction; the second inspired much poetry; . . . the first and third . . . yielded three novels written in the 1830s" (Shillingsburg, "Literary Grist" 119). This was, in part, because of the trips' timing. Sixteen years after the first trip, Simms told students at the University of Alabama that in the interval their world had changed from a howling wilderness into a place of growing civilization (Simms, *Social* 5–6). Had he not gone when he did, he would have been too late to see the frontier. Later travels took him many other places and also provided much grist for his writing. Never again, however, did he experience the frontier firsthand. Furthermore, on these later trips Simms was a practiced professional writer, no longer that boy haunted by passions.

Personal Life

After the ten-year-old boy's momentous refusal to leave Charleston, his grandmother sent Simms for two years to the grammar school taught on the campus and by the faculty of the nearly moribund College of Charleston. By then he already was "versifying the events of the war [of 1812]," just concluded, publishing "doggerel" in the local papers, and learning to read in several languages (*Letters* 1:285). His trip west a decade later helped him decide to pursue both literature and a career in law, but back in Charleston—this despite his father's urging that he stay in Mississippi. Upon his return home, he began to read law and also launched a literary weekly, the *Album*, which ran for a year. He became engaged as well to Anna Malcolm Giles, daughter of a grocer and former state coroner.

A year later the young couple married. This was six months before Simms was admitted to the South Carolina bar, on his twenty-first birthday, not long before he was appointed as a city magistrate. Although living up the Ashley River in the more healthful, less expensive village of Summerville, Simms kept a law office in the city. Shortly after using his maternal inheritance to buy the *City Gazette* at the end of 1829 and moving down to Charleston Neck, just north of the city limits where he had lived as a boy, Simms lost both his father and his maternal grandmother. He also found himself attacked because of his Unionist stance in the Nullification crisis resulting from South Carolina's rejection of a federal tariff. Then, in early 1832, Simms's wife died. Soon after, he took his four-year-old daughter back to Summerville to live and determined to sell his newspaper and leave the state for a literary life in the North.

Fueling his ambition was the correspondence Simms had begun several years earlier with an accountant whom he had published in his *City Gazette* but not yet met—Scots immigrant James Lawson. At the time Lawson, seven years Simms's senior, edited a New York City newspaper and, in addition to writing plays and poetry, was a friend (and, later, informal literary agent) to a wide circle (McHaney, "An Early"). Simms's trip north in the summer of 1832 saw the two begin a lifelong friendship, cemented as they squired ladies about and interacted with Lawson's literary circle. In subsequent years Simms multiplied the number of his friendships, in both the North and the South, making them in some measure a replacement for the family that he had lost. Lawson remained the closest of his northern friends, while James Henry Hammond, a future governor and U.S. senator, became his closest friend in South Carolina.

Late in 1833, after his Summerville house burned, Simms wrote Lawson to say that he was enamored of "a certain fair one" (*Letters* 1:73). Seventeen-year-old Chevillette Eliza Roach was the daughter of "a literary-minded aristocrat of English descent" with two plantations on the banks of the Edisto River in Barnwell District (later County) (Guilds 70). The courtship was protracted, as Simms felt it necessary first to clear debts that friends had bought up on his behalf. He also was determined "to marry no woman" before he was "perfectly independent of her resources, and her friends" (*Letters* 1:78). Therefore he did not propose until the spring of 1836. The nuptials took place seven months later, and as a result, Simms came to call the four thousand acres of Woodlands Plantation, with its seventy slaves, home. It was twenty years, however, before he took over management of the plantation and, then, only in the wake of his father-in-law's final sickness and death. Five years after that, he lost his wife, the mother of fourteen of his fifteen children. Nine of the children Chevillette bore him had already died, devastating Simms repeatedly. Five were still living (three sons and two daughters), as was Simms's daughter by his first marriage, who helped raise the youngest of her siblings. Those remaining children—even Gilly, who fought in the Confederate army—all outlived their father. Gilly and a brother-in-law ran Woodlands after the war, when Simms, though dying of cancer, was earning what he could by writing again for publications in the North and editing one or another South Carolina newspaper.

Career

The trip north in 1832 did not result in Simms moving there. Except during the Civil War, however, he returned almost every year. This was because the contacts he made, and the exposure to literary culture that he enjoyed, helped him define his future as an author. Earlier he had written fiction and criticism as well as journalism, filling the pages of several short-lived cultural journals and his newspaper, but between the ages of nine and twenty-six Simms had focused his literary efforts primarily on poetry. Beginning with his first book of verse in 1825, he had published five small volumes in Charleston. A couple had received positive notice in New York, and in the fall of 1832, J. & J. Harper issued the sixth anonymously from there, *Atalantis: A Story of the Sea.* Coming back the following summer, Simms had in hand for the Harpers a gothic novella, *Martin Faber,* and after his return south, he also would send the manuscript of his first two-volume border romance, *Guy Rivers: A Tale of Georgia.*

The reception of these and the romances and short stories that followed quickly made Simms one of the nation's most successful fictionists. He continued to issue poetry as well—roughly a collection every three years over the thirty-seven years that he worked as a professional author. But this output was dwarfed by the fiction—on average a title every year (counting several serialized works but not counting the many revised editions). Then there were the two dozen separately published orations, histories, and biographies as well as edited collections of documents and dramas and a geography of South Carolina. Add to these the revised editions and the further printings and issues of his own works and it appears that Simms saw a title coming off the presses at the rate of one every three months or so. Making that figure all the more astounding is the fact that, during more than a dozen of those years (the early-to-mid 1840s, the late 1840s-to-early 1850s, and the mid-to-late 1860s), he also was editing a cultural journal or newspaper. Furthermore he contributed reams of reviews and poems, hundreds of op-ed pieces and columns, and dozens of short stories and public addresses, which were never collected and published in volume form.

His career mapped an arc. It ascended meteorically in the 1830s and peaked in the early-to-mid 1840s, before beginning to descend. One reason was the popularity of the historical fiction that Simms began to write. When he left behind the law, his first newspaper, and the Nullification controversy, as well as his sadness, historical fiction was all the rage. Sir Walter Scott had fueled the craze, beginning with the publication of his first Border romance in 1814. He died in September 1832. Seventeen years Simms's senior, James Fenimore Cooper, the closest America had to a Scott at the time, was at the peak of his reputation and success, having started publishing his romances in 1820. Thus the way had been prepared for a writer of Simms's historical imagination and preoccupations. Within five years of his first trip north, moreover, Lawson's (and now his) circle became loosely affiliated with a nationalistic and Democratic group, self-styled Young America, this after Young Italy and similar ethnic, nationalist, European, cultural and political movements (Moltke-Hansen, "Southern"). Edgar Allan Poe and other members gave Simms's first fictions positive, if not uncritical, attention.

By the end of the 1830s, paradoxically, Simms, like Cooper, found his success attracting unauthorized editions of his works because Britain and America did not have an international copyright agreement. Further, in the wake of the panic of 1837, Americans bought fewer books. Simms's response was to diversify his portfolio. He turned to biography and history, including his hugely successful *Life of Francis Marion* (1844). He also returned to the editor's chair, overseeing one and then another cultural journal. These were unlike the ones he had edited in the 1820s: they included contributions by numerous authors, not just those from Charleston, but from the region and also the North. The ambition motivating the journals was to connect and promote Charleston intellectually. Consequently the journals more closely resembled metropolitan quarterly reviews in their offerings.

The mid-1840s saw Simms involved in politics, even serving a term in the South Carolina legislature. By the middle of the Mexican-American War in 1847, he had concluded that the South needed to become an independent nation. Thereafter, although he maintained ties with many in the Young America circle, he no longer promoted his writings as fostering Americanism in literature (*Views*). Instead he increasingly emphasized the ways in which his three romance series—the colonial, the Revolutionary, and the border—were making tangible and meaningful the origins and development of the future southern nation and the sad but inevitable consequences for Native Americans (Watson, *From Nationalism*; compare Nakamura).

Sectional politics colored more and more of Simms's perceptions, speeches, and private communications. The rising tide of abolitionism had him aghast. It also fed his growing sense that his position in American letters was slipping. He returned to editing, and his poetry, which was more often explicitly about the South, became increasingly patriotic in tone. Although his first biographer, William Peterfield Trent, insisted that Simms's declining standing reflected the change in literary fashion from historical romances to realistic novels, Simms in fact wrote more and more as a social realist in the 1850s (Wimsatt, "Realism").

The Civil War consumed Simms. As he wrote Lawson, "Literature, especially poetry, is effectually overwhelmed by the drums, & the cavalry, and the shouting" (*Letters* 4:369–70). He did manage to editorialize often and to rework and finish things long on his desk, including poems, a novel, and a dramatic treatment of Benedict Arnold, the northern traitor in the Revolutionary War. Then, in the wake of the Confederacy's loss and the failure of his vision for the South, he found himself recording the loss in a new newspaper, dealing with the trauma in his poetry, and becoming more existential and psychological in his fictional treatments. Simms's old New York friends tried to help. He did edit and see through publication a volume of Confederate war poetry. Yet it is a measure of his reduced stature that the several new romances he published appeared only in serial form. In part this may have been because he was in a sense competing with himself. Publishers were beginning to reprint volumes out of the selected edition of his writings. Many of Simms's works were available in book form, just not new works.

Associations

As the *Letters* testify, Simms had complex, overlapping networks of friends and colleagues. As a boy and young man, he received the friendship, patronage, and commendation of a variety of well-placed people in Charleston, including Charles Rivers Carroll. It was Carroll with whom he read law, to whom he dedicated his first romance, and after whom he named a son. Both men were Unionists during the Nullification controversy. So were Hugh Swinton Legare (later U.S. attorney general) and the considerably older William Drayton, as well as lawyer and editor Richard Yeadon and Greenville, South Carolina, newspaper editor Benjamin Franklin Perry. Also considerably older was James Wright Simmons, who had joined with Simms to launch the *Southern Literary Gazette* in 1828, when Simms was twenty-two. Through him Simms had direct contact with such British literary figures as Leigh Hunt and Byron (Kibler, *Poetry* 15).

The next group of influential friends and collaborators that Simms acquired were members of the Lawson circle and included such figures as Edwin

Forrest, the Shakespearean actor, and Evert Duyckinck, who published several of Simms's volumes in Wiley and Putnam's series Library of American Books, which he edited. Among the many others were poets and editors William Cullen Bryant and Fitz-Greene Halleck. Simms also made nonliterary friends in New York and Philadelphia, such as John Jacob Bockee and William Hawkins Ferris, the cashier at the U.S. Treasury office in New York who, after the war, helped Simms, Henry Timrod (poet laureate of the Confederacy), and others.

As a Barnwell planter, Simms met a widening circle of South Carolina's leaders and literati. For instance his acquaintance with James Henry Hammond began in the late 1830s and deepened into a friendship in the early 1840s. It was in the early 1840s, too, when he again was editing cultural journals, that Simms became friends with many southern writers. He regarded several of them, including Virginians George Frederick Holmes, Edmund Ruffin, and Nathaniel Beverley Tucker as members, together with Hammond and himself, in a "sacred circle." Uniting the circle were members' devotion to the South and a shared sense of the marginal status and critical importance of the life of the mind in a largely rural and unintellectual region (Faust, *Sacred*). Others of Simms's wide connections in the region did not interact as much with each other, but Simms long corresponded with Maryland novelist and lawyer John Pendleton Kennedy, Irish-born Georgia poet Richard Henry Wilde, Alabama lawyer and writer Alexander Beaufort Meek, and Louisiana historian and assistant attorney general Charles Gayarré, among others. By the 1850s, when Simms once more returned to editing a cultural journal, many of the writers whom he recruited were members of a younger generation. Poets Paul Hamilton Hayne and Henry Timrod were two. Often they and a half dozen others of Simms's and their generations met in John Russell's Charleston Book Shop and adjourned to dinner at Simms's Smith Street home, "dubbed 'The Wigwam'" (*Letters* 1:cxxxvi). Shortly before his death fifteen or so years later, Simms wrote Hayne, "I am rapidly passing from the stage, where you young men are to succeed me" (*Letters* 5:287).

Thought

The welter of Simms's works disguises unities and dynamics of the thought underlying them. From early on Simms was convinced that art ennobles or transforms, as well as gives voice to individuals and societies; therefore it must be cultivated assiduously. Without the potential for high artistic attainment, he insisted, societies are not ready for the independence and regard of free peoples. This is where Simms the historian joined Simms the poet. Societies develop, he argued (using the stadialism of the Scottish historical school), from imitation through self-assertion to achievement and also from savagery through strife to settled agricultural communities and, ultimately, to a hierarchical civilization supporting a rich artistic life. It was the job of the artist to help envision the goal, inspire the pursuit, and inform the process. That process was at once progressive and dialectical. Order, without dynamism, stifled development, as did the obverse—the dominance by ungoverned impulses or uncontrolled license. This was true in the individual, but also in societies as a whole. War was necessary for civilization, but its success was measured in the securities of the home, the center of cultural production and reproduction.

Whether in the public or in the domestic arena, "the true governor, as [Thomas] Carlyle call[ed] him—the king man—" guided rather than impeded the forces of change and progress (Simms, "Guizot's" 122). There were few such men with the capacity to lead. The same was true of nations. Neither all people nor all peoples were equal in either capacity or attainment. That was why Native Americans were overrun and Africans had been enslaved by European peoples in the New World. Indeed, Simms argued, "slavery in all ages has been found the greatest and most admirable agent of Civilization," giving education and examples to less evolved peoples (*Letters* 3:174). The degree to which a people had evolved mattered. That was why, he held, Americans had won independence from the most powerful empire in the world. They had done so through their Revolution, led by an elite that felt correctly its time had come (Simms, "Ellet's" 328). By mid-1847 that also was Simms's judgment for the South: the region had evolved enough to become independent (*Letters* 2:332). The hope inspired and then failed him and the people he sought to lead.

While not all men could rise to the highest rank, they all had the same responsibility at home. There the father was patriarch, protector, and head, while the mother was nurturer, moral instructor, and heart. There, too, children's characters and minds were formed by age twelve ("Ellet's"). Children's upbringing was critical to citizenship, and it was through her sons and the support of her husband, father, and brothers that a woman shaped the public sphere. The culture and character instilled in the child expressed and informed not just the household, but the larger society—the people.

"The history of peoples and their embodiments in institutions, states, and artistic productions—these were the great subjects" in Simms's view (Moltke-Hansen, "Southern" 120). Yet "poets were the only class of philosophers who had recognized" this until his own day, when at last "we now read human histories. We now ask after the affections as well as the ceremonies of society" ("Ellet's" 319-20). Peoples or races—that is, ethnic groups—were not unchanging any more than were their politics and their cultures. They either advanced or were overrun by history. Further, new peoples emerged, and old identities were submerged. The Spanish conquistadors were the creation of centuries of conflict with the Moors: their motivation was the glory of conquest, not the routine of trade or the plow. On the other hand, the English settlements in North America reflected the impulse to transform the wilderness into verdant farms and build society (*Views* 64, 178–85; *Social* 8). The same impulse drove Americans westward in Simms's own day and gave Americans their Manifest Destiny.

To explore these facts of the South's settlement and its place in international conflicts, Simms wrote all together, between 1833 and 1863, two romances set in eighth-century Spain, two set during the Spanish exploration and conquest of the Americas and two during the later English colonization of South Carolina, seven set during the American Revolution, and—depending on how one counts—perhaps eight set on the borders of the nineteenth-century South. After the war he published one more Revolutionary romance and two more that, like it, were set beyond the boundaries of civilization. He also left two unfinished romances, also set beyond society's normal reach. These late works, however, no longer had as their framing justification the cultivation of the South's future and civilization.

White southerners had their independence foreclosed by the war. In his last works, therefore, Simms found himself exploring the psychological, philosophical, and historical impulses that led to the Confederacy's demise and what, in the aftermath, it meant to be a good man and to build for the future, however impoverished. On the first score, he argued that the impulse to idealism behind abolitionism ignored historical realities, becoming inhuman in its consequences. On the latter score, he affirmed responsibility for one's dependents and the virtues of stoicism, as well as a continued commitment to the beauty and truth of art and the impulses to the cultivated life and fields. Therefore, in the face of the burning of his Woodlands home and library in February 1865—during Sherman's march and in the midst of desperate circumstances—he insisted that home, or the ideals and past characterizing its potential, still was at the center of true civilization, but only if elevated by art (*Sense* 8, 17). It was wrong to measure civilization by the getting, spending, and mad dashing, or material progress and utilitarianism, characteristic of both a capitalistic North and also many southerners. These traits he often had attacked even before the war, insisting that "the work of the Imagination, which is the Genius of a race, is only begun when its material progress is supposed to be complete" (*Poetry* 12).

Writings

Simms expressed many of his ideas most personally in letters and most cogently in essays, speeches, and occasional introductions to his books. But he illustrated them most fully in his fiction and poetry. By the time he arrived in New

York in 1832, he had formed many of the core ideals and beliefs that would shape his work. His application of them, however, modified his understanding over time. Growing as a writer and growing in knowledge and experience, he also grew as a thinker.

In his hierarchy of values, poetry came first. It was a prophetic calling as well as evocative of the deeply felt (or, sometimes, the fleeting) and thus testimony to the perdurance and transcendence of the beautiful and the human spirit. Yet, as Simms often ruefully reflected, prose spoke to many more people. That was a principal reason why he turned to writing prose epics or romances. He gave his most concerted consideration of poetry's value and roles in three lectures in Charleston in 1854. Over the prior three years he had given portions of them in Augusta, Georgia, Washington, D.C., and Richmond and Petersburg, Virginia. Entitled *Poetry and the Practical*, they did not see print until 1996, as Simms never found the time to expand them as he wanted. On the other hand, his last address on the same themes, *The Sense of the Beautiful*, was issued soon after he delivered it, also in Charleston.

Many of his important reviews have not yet been gathered, but Simms collected some in 1845–46, and *Views and Reviews in American Literature, History and Fiction* came out in 1846 and 1847 in two "series." Beginning with a consideration of "Americanism" in literature, the first series explored the themes and periods of American history for treatment by the novelist. Simms argued there, and in forewords to several of his romances, that fiction rendered the past more truthfully, interestingly, and tellingly than histories and biographies could because fiction—like poetry—required imagination to look beyond what is not known or expressed. The second series examined additional American writers and what distinguished them, for instance, in their humor.

Despite their early success, Simms's romances, novellas, and stories provoked mixed reviews. Poe eventually concluded that Simms had become "the best novelist which this country has, on the whole, produced" but also insisted that "he should never have written 'The Partisan,' nor 'The Yemassee.'" This was in a review of *Confession*. That novel, like the gothic *Martin Faber*, demonstrated, Poe contended, that Simms's "genius [did] not lie in the outward so much as in the inner world." Yet he nevertheless wrote of Simms's short-story collection *The Wigwam and the Cabin* that "in invention, in vigor, in movement, in the power of exciting interest, and in the artistical management of his themes, he has surpassed, we think, any of his countrymen." Other critics, especially in the genteel and Whiggish Knickerbocker circle, joined Poe in condemning what they considered to be the excessively graphic and vulgar qualities of many characters and scenes, and Simms's prolixity and sententiousness, in his romances (Butterworth and Kibler 64, 50).

The violent realism and earthiness of the romances did not result in realistic novels. Although Simms received early praise for his characterizations (particularly of women), he used the romance formula, with its stereotypic heroes and heroines, predictable themes, and conventional polarities. People were on quests or had lost their way or were fighting long odds or were carrying forward the banner of (and modeling) civilization or were mired in the slough of despond or were resisting all the claims of civilized society and behavior or were pursuing love interests. Deceitfulness, selfishness, and greed opposed honor, high-mindedness, and honesty against the backdrop of the South's development from the earliest days of Spanish exploration to the westward movement in Simms's own youth.

It was only gradually that Simms married the psychological acuity of some of his portraits of the interior struggles of his gothic characters and fiction to the historical romance. Helping him think through how to do so were the biographies he wrote in the mid-1840s, but also the incidents on which he focused particular fictions, such as the murder in *Beauchampe; or, The Kentucky Tragedy* (1842). However incomplete the blending of realism and romanticism or of stereotypical and socially individuated renderings through the 1840s, by the 1850s Simms fundamentally had made the transition to social realism in such works as *Woodcraft* and *The Cassique of Kiawah*. Indeed some scholars have considered *Woodcraft* the first realistic novel in America (Bakker; Wimsatt, "Realism").

In some sense disguising the transition is the fact that Simms also increasingly wrote as a humorist and, in so doing, often rendered his late narratives fabulistically, when not writing social comedy or stories of manners. This dimension of Simms's work was largely hidden, however, until the 1974 publication of *Stories and Tales*, volume 5 in the Centennial Simms edition. There, for the first time, readers had access in print to "Bald-Head Bill Bauldy." There, too, for the first time one could read together that story, "Legend of the Hunter's Camp," and "How Sharp Snaffles Got His Capital and Wife," which was published posthumously in *Harper's Magazine* in October 1870. These and other stories and tales made it clear that Simms was a fecund contributor to southern and American humor.

Humor let Simms take up issues that he could not otherwise address in print and still expect to be well received. He did so both during and after the war. The war also pushed Simms past the emerging fashion of social realism. Having destroyed the familiar, the preoccupation of much realistic fiction, the war made the liminal central (Shillingsburg, "Cub"). While his romances and tales had often explored life on the edge or in extreme circumstances, whether in war or on the frontier or on the verge of madness or in fanciful realms, it had done so against a backdrop of, and with the goal of affirming, social norms and development. In the war's wake that goal seemed absurd. Mythologized memories of a healthy past might nurture a sense of the beautiful but could not help one deal with the present. Thus Simms's conclusion, in a March 1869 letter to Paul Hamilton Hayne: "Let us bury the Past lest it buries us!" (*Letters* 5:214). Fifteen months later he lay dead in the 13 Society Street, Charleston, home of his oldest daughter, with the shell holes in the walls of the bedroom he had shared with several children.

Posthumous Reputation

The twenty years after Simms's death saw him often respectfully treated, first in obituaries, later in memoirs and columns, and also in literary dictionaries and encyclopedias. Yet Charles Richardson's 1887 *American Literature: 1607–1885* proved a harbinger of a shift: Simms, Richardson observed, was "more respected than read," having "won considerable note because he was so sectional" and then having "lost it because he was not sectional enough," although he showed "silly contempt for his Northern betters" (qtd. in Butterworth and Kibler 130). Five years later Trent's biography of Simms appeared. It was the first full-length, scholarly treatment. Its central thesis was that Simms's environment frustrated his abilities: the South was inimical to art and the life of the mind, and Charleston high society's hauteur marginalized Simms despite his talent and character. Trent's second thesis was that Simms's commitment to the romance and his romanticism meant that his works had become largely unreadable in an age of literary realism. Although Vernon Parrington and later scholars recognized Simms's impulses to realism, the two theses long shaped Simms criticism and, indeed, also helped frame study of antebellum southern literature and intellectual life (Parrington 119–30).

A Virginian born in 1862, Trent was a progressive who wanted a New South radically different from the old. He saw his pioneering study of Simms as an opportunity to criticize what the Civil War had made untenable. From his perspective the Old South was not the expanding and rapidly developing environment, with a deep history, that Simms portrayed, but a place where slavery stultified and stunted the growth and progress displayed by the North. Southern—especially South Carolinian—writers occasionally challenged Trent's agenda and conclusions, but those critiques had little impact. Not until after publication of the Simms letters in the 1950s did scholars begin to consider the author in the historical and contemporary contexts that he had rendered in his poetry and fiction. And not until after the centennial of his death did a growing number of scholars, having concluded that southern intellectual history was not an oxymoron, begin to study in detail the culture in which Simms participated and to which he contributed so voluminously and variously.

Some of these scholars also have had agendas: they have wanted to see Simms included in the American literary canon, for instance, or they have wanted to defend the heritage that in their view Trent, and so many others, inappropriately belittled or ignorantly dismissed. More fruitfully, other scholars have begun to reframe the understanding of nineteenth-century American intellectual life by stripping away preconceptions that characterized earlier evaluations of Simms and his contemporaries. They are closely examining the historical record and transatlantic and other contemporary contexts and developments in the process. Although the pursuit of canonical status in a post-canonical age seems quixotic at this point, the explosion of the canon is leading to more varied fare being offered and may, therefore, mean that Simms, once his work is widely available, will be more often anthologized as well as studied. Defensiveness about Simms and the antebellum South may warm the hearts of like-minded people, just as critics of the Old South have been encouraged by shared presuppositions and disdain. Yet dueling cultural ideologies do not advance comity and may only reinforce mutual incomprehensions. Continued, deep research in original sources and the theoretical reframing that Atlantic history, the history of the book, and other perspectives offer — these approaches promise most for further study of Simms, his works, and his world.

Works Cited

For amplified readings by and on Simms and on his world, go to http://simms.library.sc.edu/bibliography.php.

Bakker, Jan. "Simms on the Literary Frontier; or, So Long Miss Ravenel and Hello Captain Porgy: *Woodcraft* Is the First 'Realistic' Novel in America." In *William Gilmore Simms and the American Frontier,* edited by John Caldwell Guilds and Caroline Collins, 64–78. Athens: University of Georgia Press, 1997.

Butterworth, Keen, and James E. Kibler Jr. *William Gilmore Simms: A Definitive Guide.* Boston: G. K. Hall, 1980.

Faust, Drew Gilpin. *A Sacred Circle: The Dilemma of the Intellectual in the Old South, 1840–1860.* Baltimore: Johns Hopkins University Press, 1977.

Guilds, John C. *Simms: A Literary Life.* Fayetteville: University of Arkansas Press, 1992.

Hayne, Paul Hamilton. "Ante-Bellum Charleston." *Southern Bivouac* 1 (October 1885): 257–68.

Kibler, James E. "The First Simms Letters: 'Letters from the West' (1826)." *Southern Literary Journal* 19 (Spring 1987): 81–91.

———. *The Poetry of William Gilmore Simms: An Introduction and Bibliography.* Columbia: Southern Studies Program, University of South Carolina, 1979.

McHaney, Thomas L. "An Early 19th-Century Literary Agent: James Lawson of New York." *Publications of the Bibliographical Society of America* 64 (Spring 1970): 177–92.

Moltke-Hansen, David. "The Expansion of Intellectual Life: A Prospectus." In *Intellectual Life in Antebellum Charleston,* edited by Michael O'Brien and David Moltke-Hansen, 3–44. Knoxville: University of Tennessee Press, 1986.

———. "Southern Literary Horizons in Young America: Imaginative Development of a Regional Geography." *Studies in the Literary Imagination* 42, no. 1 (2009): 1–31.

Nakamura, Masahiro. *Visions of Order in William Gilmore Simms: Southern Conservatism and the Other American Romance.* Columbia: University of South Carolina Press, 2009.

Parrington, Vernon L. *The Romantic Revolution in America, 1800–1860.* Vol. 2 of *Main Currents in American Thought.* New York: Harcourt, Brace and Company, 1927.

Rogers, George C., Jr. *Charleston in the Age of the Pinckneys.* Columbia: University South Carolina Press, 1980.

Shillingsburg, Miriam J. "The Cub of the Panther: A New Frontier." In *William Gilmore Simms and the American Frontier,* edited by John Caldwell Guilds and Caroline Collins, 221–36. Athens: University of Georgia Press, 1997.

———. "Literary Grist: Simms's Trips to Mississippi." *Southern Quarterly* 41, no. 2 (2003): 119–34.

Simms, William Gilmore. *Atalantis: A Story of the Sea: In Three Parts.* New York: J. & J. Harper, 1832.

———. *Beauchampe; or, The Kentucky Tragedy.* 2 vols. Philadelphia: Lea and Blanchard, 1842.

———. *The Cassique of Kiawah: A Colonial Romance.* New York: Redfield, 1859.

———. *Confession; or, The Blind Heart. A Domestic Story.* 2 vols. Philadelphia: Lea and Blanchard, 1841.

———. "Ellet's 'Women of the Revolution.'" *Southern Quarterly Review,* n.s. 1 (July 1850): 314–54.

———. "Guizot's Democracy in France." *Southern Quarterly Review* 15, no.29 (1849): 114–65.

———. *Guy Rivers: A Tale of Georgia.* 2 vols. New York: Harper & Brothers, 1834.

———. *The Letters of William Gilmore Simms.* Edited by Mary C. Simms Oliphant, Alfred Taylor Odell, and T. C. Duncan. 6 vols. Columbia: University of South Carolina Press, 1952–82.

———. *The Life of Francis Marion.* New York: Henry G. Langley, 1844.

———. *Martin Faber, the Story of a Criminal; and Other Tales.* 2 vols. New York: Harper & Brothers, 1837.

———. *Poetry and the Practical.* Edited by James E. Kibler. Fayetteville: University of Arkansas Press, 1996.

———. *The Sense of the Beautiful: An Address . . . before the Charleston County Agricultural and Horticultural Association, May 3, 1870.* Charleston: Charleston County Agricultural and Horticultural Association, 1870.

---. *The Social Principle: The Source of National Permanence. An Oration, Delivered before the Erosophic Society of the University of Alabama . . . December 13, 1842.* Tuscaloosa: Erosophic Society, University of Alabama, 1843.

---. *Stories and Tales.* Vol. 5 of *The Writings of William Gilmore Simms.* Centennial edition; introductions, explanatory notes, and texts established by John Caldwell Guilds. Columbia: University of South Carolina Press, 1974.

---. *Views and Reviews in American Literature, History and Fiction.* 2 vols. New York: Wiley and Putnam, 1845 (1846).

---. *The Wigwam and the Cabin.* 2 vols. New York: Wiley and Putnam, 1845–46.

---. *Woodcraft, or Hawks about the Dovecote: A Story of the South, at the Close of the Revolution.* New York: Redfield, 1854.

Trent, William Peterfield. *William Gilmore Simms.* Boston: Houghton, Mifflin, 1892.

Wakelyn, Jon L. *The Politics of a Literary Man: William Gilmore Simms.* Westport, Conn.: Greenwood Press, 1973.

Watson, Charles S. *From Nationalism to Secessionism: The Changing Fiction of William Gilmore Simms.* Westport, Conn.: Greenwood Press, 1993.

White, William B., Jr. *The Ross-Chesnut-Sutton Family of South Carolina.* Franklin, N.C.: Privately printed, 2002.

Wimsatt, Mary Ann. "Realism and Romance in Simms's Midcentury Fiction." *Southern Literary Journal* 12, no. 2 (1980): 29–48.

Critical Introduction

THE GEOGRAPHY OF SOUTH CAROLINA

Sean R. Busick

William Gilmore Simms's *The History of South Carolina* was first published by Charleston's S. Babcock and Company in 1840, bearing the rather cumbersome title *The History of South Carolina, from Its First European Discovery to Its Erection into a Republic: With a Supplementary Chronicle of Events to the Present Time*. Two years later Simms revised the book. Then in 1843 he published his *The Geography of South Carolina*, also with S. Babcock and Company. It was intended to be a supplement to the *History*. On the eve of the Civil War, Simms again revised and updated the *History*. This expanded and revised 1860 edition was published by New York's Redfield. Between the first edition of 1840 and the 1860 revision, the book grew from 319 pages to 437 pages.[1]

Unlike Simms's other books the *History* and *The Geography of South Carolina* were written primarily as textbooks for young students. He feared that the majority of South Carolinians, young and old alike, were largely ignorant of their state's history: "To say that the great majority of our young people know little or nothing of the history of the state, is to do them no injustice. We may equally charge this deficiency upon the old." (*History*, 1860 ed. 5)[2] Simms hoped to fill this need with a history that could serve as a textbook, while also appealing to interested older readers — a textbook that would be a pleasure rather than a chore to read. "I am now writing a History of South Carolina in a single volume, intended for the use of schools and for the general reader, who in these piping times, eschews heedfully all ponderous quartos," he wrote to his friend James Lawson on 20 July 1839. (*Letters* 1: 151) As John C. Guilds, Simms's biographer, has observed, "Since South Carolina historical data substantially provide the basis for the Revolutionary Romances and other fiction, Simms's assuming the role of historian per se was not an abrupt departure" from the sort of work he had been writing throughout his career (Guilds 93-94).

In his preface to the *History*, Simms explained that the idea for the book came to him when he began to teach his thirteen year old daughter Augusta her state's history. It was then that he discovered that no existing book was suitable to his purposes. One problem with many of the existing state histories, was that they were "so cumbrous, and so loaded as they are with prolix disquisition, and unnecessary if not irrelevant detail," that they were inappropriate for "the unprepared understanding and the ardent temper of the young." The available state histories were simply too long and too dull for Simms's purposes. An unread, or unreadable, book did no one any good. The older histories tended to be encumbered with dry and dated political discourses on topics that were no longer of interest to the state's readers. "To the great portion of the reading community they are entirely useless," he wrote. (*History* 2)

The excessive length of the existing state histories, with many running to two volumes, also rendered them too expensive to reach a wide audience. Simms believed authors and publishers had a responsibility to make quality books available to the masses by producing inexpensive literature: "Books for schools and for the popular reader—the two objects for which the present history is designed—must be cheap as well as compact." With this goal and his intended audience in mind, Simms left out footnote references and all "unnecessary details," and tried to avoid excessive "prolixity" (*History* 3). He also scaled the project back as far as he thought he could, limiting himself to a relatively small one-volume history and a separate geography of the state. "In separating the political and social from the geographical history of the state" he wrote in the preface to *Geography*, "the object was to simplify the subject, and so to preserve unbroken the stream of narrative in the former work, as to make its perusal by the youthful reader, a pleasure rather than a task" (iii). What he believed was needed, was "to place the facts in a simple form, in a just order; to give them an expressive and energetic character; to couple events closely, so that no irrelevant or unnecessary matter should interpose itself between the legitimate relation of cause and effect; and to be careful that the regular stream of the narrative should flow on without interruption to the end of its course" (*History* 6). Simms was confident that a history and geography written according to this plan could accomplish much good in educating the public.

The Geography of South Carolina draws heavily from the work of Robert Mills, America's first professional architect and the designer of the Washington Monument. Mills also compiled an atlas of South Carolina which is still the most comprehensive source for geographical information on the state in the early nineteenth century. Simms's geography text might more accurately be thought of as a natural history of South Carolina; he wrote and organized it according to the conventions of natural history. This peculiarly American literary genre developed out of the need to systematically describe a vast new continent. It included the writings of John and William Bartram, Thomas Jefferson, John Filson, and many others with whose works Simms was familiar. Natural history would later engage the talents of writers ranging from Henry David Thoreau to Wendell Berry. Like countless earlier descriptions of America,

Simms's *Geography of South Carolina* begins by surveying the state's physical extent, then moves on to enumerate its physical features, its flora, and its fauna, before describing its human inhabitants and their higher political and cultural attainments.[3]

Instead of a bibliography, Simms acknowledged his debt to several authors in *The History of South Carolina*'s preface. Those authors included Bartholomew Rivers Carroll Jr., Alexander Hewatt, John Drayton, David Ramsay, William Moultrie, William Johnson, George Bancroft, William J. Rivers, Banastre Tarleton, "and several others" (*History* 5). He quoted freely from these authors, and though the quotes are not cited in footnotes, the text generally makes clear the source of quotations.

It is also worth noting that Simms used his sources critically, as any good historian must. When they were wrong or inconsistent, he did not hesitate to point this out to the reader. In one instance, for example, he noted that, according to some sources, "South Carolina was estimated to contain ninety-three thousand whites [at the time of the Revolution], when she could not possibly have contained sixty thousand" (*History* 199). In another instance, he pointed out what he believed was an error on the part of some historians who had said that General Nathanael Greene had been caught off guard by the Lord Rawdon at Hobkirk's Hill in April 1781 (*History* 299). And he was not afraid to admit his uncertainty when his research failed conclusively to settle an issue in dispute. "All the clues to argument upon doubtful or disputed points have been indicated," he told his readers (*History* 6). Because of that and of his extensive research, Simms believed his own *The History of South Carolina* was "in many respects original, especially in the suggestion of clues; and it embodies much material which has escaped other historians" (*History* 6). Upon completing *The History* Simms could confidently write to his friend James Lawson on 25 October 1840 that "there is no Romance about it" — unlike some of his other books (*Letters* 1: 194).

His original research involved poring over all the relevant manuscripts in his extensive private collection and others that he could get access to, traveling to all portions of the state to see historic sites firsthand, and corresponding with authorities on local history. One such research trip was planned for the summer of 1847 to familiarize himself with the scenery, history, and manners of the upcountry for a revision to the *History*. Simms wrote in May 1847 to John C. Calhoun that he hoped to take a summer "jaunt" in South Carolina's mountains. "My purpose will be to pick up as much historical material as possible in relation to the events of the revolution in the interior, so that I may make my History of the State more complete, and more satisfactory to the upper country" (*Letters* 2: 318-19). In planning the trip he sought the assistance of Greenville's Benjamin F. Perry who was knowledgeable about upcountry Revolutionary history. "I am thinking of a new Edition of my History of South Carolina, in which I propose to incorporate all the matter that can be procured in regard to the up country history," he explained to Perry, "In this work I shall look to you for assistance" (*Letters* 2: 317). Simms's itinerary included the Cowpens and King's Mountain battlefields, and he hoped Perry would share his knowledge of local Revolutionary history and lore (*Letters* 2: 330, 333). As a result of this diligent research and careful revising, Simms felt confident that impartial readers of his last revised edition of the *History* would agree that he had "suffered nothing, by way of clue, suggestion, argument, or fact, to escape me" (*Letters* 4: 187).

The two main lessons of the book are that South Carolinians ought always to depend on native leadership and that they ought also to present a united front against external foes. These points are driven home in Simms's telling of the story of the American Revolution in the state. Though not strictly limited in scope to the War for Independence, *The History of South Carolina* deals extensively with the Revolution, and it is one of his most important treatments of the war. In the 1860 edition, 237 of the 437 pages are devoted to the story of the Revolution and the events from 1765 leading up to it. The American Revolution is the focus and central theme of the narrative. In fact, the full title Simms chose for the book indicates that the history of South Carolina culminates in the Revolution and the state's "erection" into a republic; subsequent events were mere epilogue.

As was the case with his other works on the Revolution, Simms sought to describe the war in South Carolina accurately, in a lively manner, to reach as large an audience as possible. In his narrative the Revolution is portrayed as the product of a long progress of social and ideological forces that nurtured and developed the colonies until they were ready for independence. Simms depicted the Revolution in South Carolina as a fratricidal civil war that was exacerbated by ethnic divisions within the colony, and much of the credit for the eventual victory, he emphasized, was due to irregular forces of partisans and militia. If *The History of South Carolina* can truly be said to have a thesis, it is that unity is essential in times of crisis and that South Carolina had been fortunate to have capable native leaders to see it through every emergency.

According to Simms, the Revolution began in South Carolina in October 1765 when the decision was made to resist the Stamp Act (*History* 158).[4] Previous to this tax, South Carolina had little reason for discontent with the mother country: "She had, on the contrary, many good reasons for loving her with undeviating loyalty." She enjoyed the protection of British arms and fleets and profited by her mercantile connection with the mother country. South Carolians suffered lightly, if at all, under "the array of evils, wrongs, and abuses" that afflicted the northern colonies that had more substantial manufacturing and shipping interests (*History* 152, 153). Instead of finding herself in competition with English economic interests, South Carolina benefited from her connection with England: "She provided the raw material which the other manufactured, and she received the manufactured goods in exchange for her productions. The intercourse was simple enough between them, and the occasions for conflict were few and unimportant" (*History* 202). Neither had she felt the oppressiveness of British arms. On the contrary, British "men, money, and munitions" protected South Carolina from hostile Native Americans and Spaniards (*History* 181). Her causes of quarrel were not economic as much as sympathy with the plight of Massachusetts and chafing at British arrogance and the denial of a few abstract principles. "The duties on tea and stamped paper were not felt, regarding the amount; but as the assertion of an authority adverse to the rights of the people and the province," Simms explained (*History* 180).

South Carolina and Great Britain were bound not only by self-interest but also by an affection grown from sharing a language, a similar culture, and many of the same traditions. South Carolina's constitution and government were based on British models, and many of her citizens worshipped at Anglican churches and enjoyed reading English literature: "The people were especially fond of British tastes, manners, and opinions; their children had a British education, and they spoke of the mother-country invariably under the endearing appellation of 'home.'" They also inherited "the natural spirit of liberty and right which fills the bosom of an English stock" (*History* 152, 153).

South Carolinians considered themselves Englishmen, possessed of the rights of Englishmen. These rights had always been jealously guarded, and they never shrank from asserting them. South Carolinians overthrew the colony's Lord Proprietors in 1719 for abusing the colonists' rights. Indeed, Simms believed that "the whole progress of the province of South Carolina had been calculated to nourish a spirit of independence among the people." Trial and strife had both strengthened them and made them aware of their strength. Most white colonists were freehold farmers who recognized no superiors, and "agriculture had taught them simplicity, hardihood, and a frank, bold, free speech and thought" (*History* 154). South Carolinians had no aristocracy and knew no restraints on their exercise of religion. Even slavery tended to make them more jealous of their own liberties while heightening their own sense of dignity. As the colony grew in population and wealth the colonists grew in local pride and boldness and were less content to be governed by a distant foreign court.

The period that witnessed Carolina's astounding growth and prosperity was an interval of salutary neglect during the reigns of George I and II that had fostered self-government and conditioned her citizens to expect little royal or parliamentary interference in their affairs. "The ascent of George the Third to the throne brought with it a change of policy in Britain, and with regard to the province, which awakened the anxieties of the intelligent and aroused the fears of the vigilant and jealous," Simms observed (*History* 148). Unfortunately for the cause of imperial rule, the cessation of salutary neglect coincided with the successful termination of the Seven Years' War, which removed the most dangerous threats to the colony's peace and safety. Then, free from foreign pressure, South Carolinians could begin to calculate the cost of union with England. Once this inquiry had begun, they "soon arrived at those convictions of political truth, law, and equity, which learned to question the tenure of foreign authority, and the legitimacy of these relations with the mother-country, which placed the provincials wholly at her mercy." From here, "The summits of republican freedom were not far from sight" (*History* 136).

After repeal of the Stamp Act, London tried again and again to increase the revenue from the North American colonies through the now familiar litany of taxes. These only served to confirm Americans' suspicions of imperial designs against their liberty and to widen the rift between the colonies and the court. Gradually, South Carolinians reached the conclusion that their interests and liberties would be safer in an independent American republic. Though they suffered relatively little compared to the people of Boston, they actively sympathized with their fellow colonists and saw in Boston's plight a real danger to their own liberty. In no colony, Simms wrote, was sympathy for Boston more passionately felt and expressed than in South Carolina. As Carolinians recognized, the unrestrained power that was allowed to subjugate one colony could subjugate them all. Safety could be found only in unity and concerted resistance to tyranny (*History* 160-61).

What was true for the colonies as a whole was also true for South Carolina. But her ethnic and cultural diversity spoiled hopes of internal unity against the external enemy. The colony's population contained large numbers of English, Scottish, Irish, Germans, and French Huguenots who brought their national prejudices to America and who were further divided by economic and geographic interests. Inhabitants of the backcountry for instance, had little in common with those who lived in the lowcountry. In the backcountry "a large portion of the people were foreigners, born British subjects, had been only eight or ten years in the country, had no intercourse, no sympathies, with the people of the seaboard, and were particularly jealous and resentful of the superiority which they asserted in arts, refinements, wealth, and education" (*History* 151).

Having only lived in America for a short period many of them had not developed local attachments stronger than their ties to the mother country. And they certainly felt little loyalty to the haughty lowcountry Carolinians whom Simms's narrative places in the lead of the revolutionary movement.

In the backcountry also were large Scottish and German communities which provided many Loyalists. National differences among immigrants were compounded by the fact that they tended to settle mainly in close-knit communities, maintaining their language and customs and having little intercourse with outsiders. Simms wrote, "Here, in one place, were Scotch, loyal, intense in their loyalty, and stubborn in their prejudices." In another were Irish, "more eager, enthusiastic, impulsive, somewhat reckless, and never remarkable for their loyalty to the English dominion." In other places were German, Swiss, and French Huguenot settlements. The Germans were often loyal to the Hanoverian monarch on Britain's throne; many of them having been convinced by Loyalists that rebellion meant the forfeiture of their royal grants of land. The French, like the Irish, were relatively quick to amalgamate and held little sympathy for England (*History* 142-43, 183).

The antipathy of the colonists in the interior for the coastal leaders in rebellion furnished another reason for loyalty and disharmony. In fact, backcountry farmers often viewed the lowcountry planters in much the same way that American Whigs viewed the governing aristocrats in London. If America was the periphery to London's metropolitan center, then the South Carolina backcountry could with equal justice be regarded as the periphery to the metropolitan center in Charlestown. Seeking supporters of the crown in the backcountry, Loyalist leaders successfully appealed to the "natural jealousies" and "prejudices" of poorer settlers "against rank and wealth, the haughty assumptions of the citizens and planters of the seaboard, and their free expenditure of the public money." Whig complaints against virtual representation or taxation without representation did not resonate among interior settlers. They had the same complaint against the lowcountry: "The upper settlements had been little considered by the popular leaders, in the whole progress of the revolutionary proceedings; had been, until a recent period, unrepresented in their congresses and public meetings; and, but few efforts had been made to conciliate the more talented and influential of their leading men." Neglect of their interests, and fear that cavalier rebel leaders intended to dragoon them and their sons into service, earned the Whigs many bitter enemies who had not already embraced loyalty out of affection for the crown (*History* 179-80, 182).

Yet opinion in the lowcountry was also fiercely divided. In the early stages of the Revolution, a large portion of the mercantile community attempted to remain aloof out of concern that an active engagement in politics might be bad for business — "trade being always reluctant to peril capital upon the caprices of politics." Nevertheless, when eventually forced to choose sides, "they showed themselves in their true colors, as bigoted loyalists, hostile to all popular proceedings, a danger in the very heart of the commonwealth" (*History* 151).

Despite his description of certain loyal merchants as "bigoted," Simms's treatment of the Loyalists is relatively more charitable than that offered by many of his contemporaries. In his assessment, the Loyalists were wrong and stood in the way of progress. Generally, they failed to see the full picture, and sometimes this was because they were blinded by their own selfish interests, as in the case of the aforementioned merchants. Other times, however, loyalty sprang from pure convictions. As has already been shown, many colonists were reluctant to sever ties with Britain by virtue of having not long lived in South Carolina or because they were more afraid of a potentially tyrannical power in Charlestown than in London. Others simply did not feel oppressed and therefore found the arguments for independence unconvincing. After all, "South Carolina had, indeed, been a favorite plantation of the crown, and the reluctance of thousands to sever the friendly bands which had linked them together, was not less honorable to their principles, than natural to their affections" (*History* 181).

Simms's analysis of the divisions within South Carolina closely follows that of David Ramsay, one of the first historians of the Revolution, and has been confirmed by later historians as well. Ramsay wrote that "Country religion, local policy, as well as private views, operated in disposing the inhabitants to take different sides" (Ramsay 625).[5] The Irish generally favored independence. The Scotch were disposed to loyalty, as were backcountry settlers.

There were strong arguments in favor of loyalty and, as far as Simms was concerned, adherence to one's convictions did not make one a villain. He did not doubt that "many of the loyalists were persons of little principle ... but, that the people who were subsequently degraded, under the general and opprobrious term of 'tories,' were, in many instances, moved only by an honest and loyal, if not a wise and just sense of duty." They may have been less far-sighted than their adversaries, but if their loyalty was based on honest motives the Loyalists were no less respectable (*History* 181).

Not only were the Loyalists, as described by Simms, not necessarily men with black hearts, they also did not necessarily have feeble minds. In fact, "the loyalists possessed numerous citizens of talents and real worth, who might have been conciliated, at least, to acquiesce in the movement which they might yet refuse to lead" (*History* 180). That they were not conciliated was due to the imprudence and indiscretion of patriot leaders. Unfortunately for South Carolina, individuals of both parties were guilty of indiscretions which made the conflict between them all the more harsh. Consequently, "the gulf through which they had to wade, to sympathy and union in the end, was one that dyed their garments in blood, the stains of which, to this day, are scarcely obliterated" (*History* 182).

Because South Carolina's heterogeneous population was so sharply divided within her borders, the Revolution more closely resembled a civil war than a war against a foreign foe. She "became one vast and bloody battlefield, in which nearly all of her sons contended," Simms wrote. "Unhappily," the citizens of South Carolina "too often contended with one another; and it is with a sentiment of profoundest melancholy that we record the fact, that the direst issues that ever took place within her borders ... were those in which her own sons were pitted against each other." This war was especially savage, with both sides guilty of atrocities, and, moreover, it was utterly unlike anything experienced in the northern colonies (*History* 297-98, 216).

This sort of warfare, in a sparsely settled country, was particularly suited to the operation of small bands of guerrillas. In one of those fortuitous catastrophes that sometimes occur in war, South Carolina's defense was left to her militia after the capture of Charlestown and the defeat of the Continental Army under General Gates at Camden in 1780. Ill-equipped, badly outnumbered, and with the British and their Loyalist allies in possession of the most important posts, the militia fought a partisan war against their enemy.

Simms attributed much of the militia's success to their habit of serving under leaders of their own choosing, who like the citizen-soldiers they commanded were natives of South Carolina, knowing intimately her land and people. Local partisan leaders such as Marion, Sumter, and Pickens met with greater success than generals Lincoln and Gates, who held national commissions, partly because they had "a better knowledge of the temper, character, and interests of those whom they would lead, and a proper knowledge of the soil, the situation and circumstances of the country which they undertook to defend." Therefore, they were better able to adapt their tactics to their circumstances than were either national or British commanders. Lacking local knowledge, "commanders, otherwise brave and skilful [*sic*], have led thousands of gallant men to defeat, whom a better judgement [*sic*] and a native genius might have led to victory" (*History* 224).

For Simms, South Carolina's greatest partisan leader was Francis Marion. He boldly yet cautiously led his little band of men through the swamps and forests, tirelessly harassing his foe, only giving battle when it was advantageous. By these means he succeeded in disrupting British communications and supplies, forced the dispersal of British forces over the countryside, cheered independence-minded Carolinians, and extorted from the enemy "a bloody toll at every passage through swamp, thicket, or river." Marion was so successful, Simms argued, because, through his familiarity with his native state and her citizens, he employed tactics which were "peculiarly adapted to the peculiarities in Carolina, and consequently to the genius of her people" (*History* 267). Given adequate supplies and a suitable leader, like Marion, South Carolina's militia showed itself a match for the best drilled European regulars (*History* 256-57, 325).

With both the worsening sectional conflict and the young readers for whom he wrote *The History of South Carolina* undoubtedly in mind, Simms closed the 1860 edition by noting that South Carolina had never lacked men like Marion, equal to the challenge of leading her through any trial. "We have every reason to hope and believe," he confidently wrote, "that she will never be deficient in the men who are to wield her power, assert and maintain her arguments, and defend her rights" (*History* 436-37). Simms believed South Carolina's citizens had always been one of her greatest resources, and he thought this would continue to be true.

Yet, with more than a hint of foreboding he listed in the 1860 edition those leaders his state had recently lost:

> It is with a mournful pride that we refer to the great names, in recent periods, which she has possessed and lost. [John C.] Calhoun, [George] McDuffie, [Langdon] Cheves, [Robert Y.] Hayne, [James] Hamilton [Jr.], [Thomas] Cooper, [William] Drayton, [Hugh Swinton] Legaré, [Thomas S.] Grimké, [Stephen] Elliot[t] — these are names of men equal to all the exigencies of a people, and capable of conferring fame upon any annals. They are gone! and South Carolina stands upon the threshold of a new era, and, we trust in God, a yet superior progress! Let us hope that each season shall produce its proper men. (*History* 437)

It is interesting to note here that Simms had once looked forward to Calhoun's passing, thinking that the void he left would be filled by younger men of equal, if not greater, abilities. Indeed, many of the men he listed at one time or another, most notably during the nullification crisis, were counted among Simms's political opponents. Nevertheless, he believed the talent and character possessed by these men, who inherited a tradition of patriotism and public service passed down through the Pinckneys, Rutledges, and Gadsdens, as well as Moultrie, Marion, Sumter, Laurens, and Pickens, proved the worth of studying history and "that the example of the past has not been chronicled in vain" (*History*, 1840 ed. 318). Perhaps one day, Simms seemed to suggest, some of his young readers' names could be added to the list. With an eye on the worsening sectional controversies, he hoped to inspire his readers' patriotism in anticipation of a renewed independence movement.

The History of South Carolina sold well and received favorable reviews in the press. A justly proud Simms wrote to James Lawson on 27 July 1840, "My History of South Carolina is published & promises to be very popular. I will send you a copy. The newspapers speak in flattering language, & individuals of worth, here & there do me honor in referring to it. The prospect is strong that it will answer the purpose for which it was designed, and become a school book throughout the state; in which event I shall probably have no reason to regard my labor as unproductive" (*Letters* 1: 179-80). According to a reviewer in the *Southern Quarterly Review*, "Dr. Simms' History of South-Carolina, is pronounced, by competent judges, the best history of the State, in a narrow compass, that has hitherto been published." This reviewer believed that Simms would "do the State more service" by his *History* and *Geography of South Carolina* "than by all the novels — and they are not a few — that he has written." He recommended Simms's *History* and *Geography* not only to South Carolinians, but also as an example to authors who might undertake to write school histories of their own states: "We commend them to critics, historians and teachers, for a candid judgment, and — on our own responsibility — we commend them to authors in other States, who are interested in the cause of education, as unexceptionable models for similar works, to be prepared by themselves; and to parents in South-Carolina, generally, we commend them as worthy of patronage," he wrote ("History of South-Carolina" 249). *DeBow's Review* praised the revised history as a "work of industrious research and sterling merit" (Heriott 658). The public and critical reception appeared poised to fulfill Simms's hopes for the volume.

Much to Simms's disappointment, *The History of South Carolina* was not adopted by the legislature for use in schools. This is not to say, however, that he was dissatisfied with his work, only with the legislature's failure to adopt it. As he told William Porcher Miles, he believed it was as "necessary to the public man, as to the pupil" (*Letters* 4: 186-87). Certainly he would be satisfied to know that in 1917, long after his death, his granddaughter Mrs. Mary C. Simms Oliphant heavily revised the book and, in this form, won its adoption for use in the state's public schools. *The New Simms History of South Carolina* went through multiple printings and editions, and remained in use by schools into the latter twentieth century. Thus, indirectly, Simms's work helped several generations of South Carolina schoolchildren learn their state's history.[6]

Notes

1. See Busick.

2. Unless otherwise noted, all citations are to the 1860 edition of *The History of South Carolina*.

3. For the history and organization of American natural history writing, see Regis.

4. It is worthy of note that Simms's description of South Carolina's road to independence in the *History of South Carolina* does not differ substantially from the summary of the Revolution written over 100 years later by George C. Rogers, Jr. (Rogers 30)

5. See also Weir.

6. Differing definitions of precisely what a "public" school is make satisfactory numbers difficult to come by, but according to one estimate there were 746 "public" schools serving 9,061 students in South Carolina in 1826, and 757 schools serving 20,716 students in 1860. (Wallace 460, 464)

Works Cited

Busick, Sean R. *A Sober Desire for History: William Gilmore Simms as Historian*. Columbia: U of South Carolina P, 2005.

Guilds, John C. *Simms: A Literary Life*. Fayetteville: U of Arkansas P, 1992.

Heriott, Edwin. "Education at the South." *DeBow's Review* 21.6 (1856): 650-659.

"The History of South-Carolina." *Southern Quarterly Review* 4.7 (1843): 247-249.

Ramsay, David. *History of the American. Revolution*, vol. 2. Indianapolis: Liberty Fund, Inc., 1990.

Regis, Pamela. *Describing Early America: Bartram, Jefferson, Crèvecoeur, and the Influence of Natural History*. Philadelphia: U. of Pennsylvania P. 1999.

Rogers, George C., Jr. *A South Carolina Chronology, 1497-1970*. Columbia: U of South Carolina P, 1973.

Simms, William Gilmore. *The Geography of South Carolina: Being a Companion to the History of that State*. Charleston: S. Babcock and Co., 1843.

———. *The History of South Carolina, from Its First European Discovery to Its Erection into a Republic: With a Supplementary Chronicle of Events to the Present Time*. Charleston: S. Babcock and Co., 1840.

———. *The History of South Carolina, from Its First European Discovery to Its Erection into a Republic: With a Supplementary Book, Bringing the Narrative Down to the Present Time*. New York: Redfield, 1860.

———. *The Letters of William Gilmore Simms*. Ed. Mary C. Simms Oliphant et al. 6 vols. Columbia: U of South Carolina P, 1952-2012.

Wallace, David Duncan. *South Carolina: A Short History, 1520-1948*. Chapel Hill: U of North Carolina P, 1951.

Weir, Robert M. *Colonial South Carolina: A History*. Millwood, NY: KTO P, 1983.

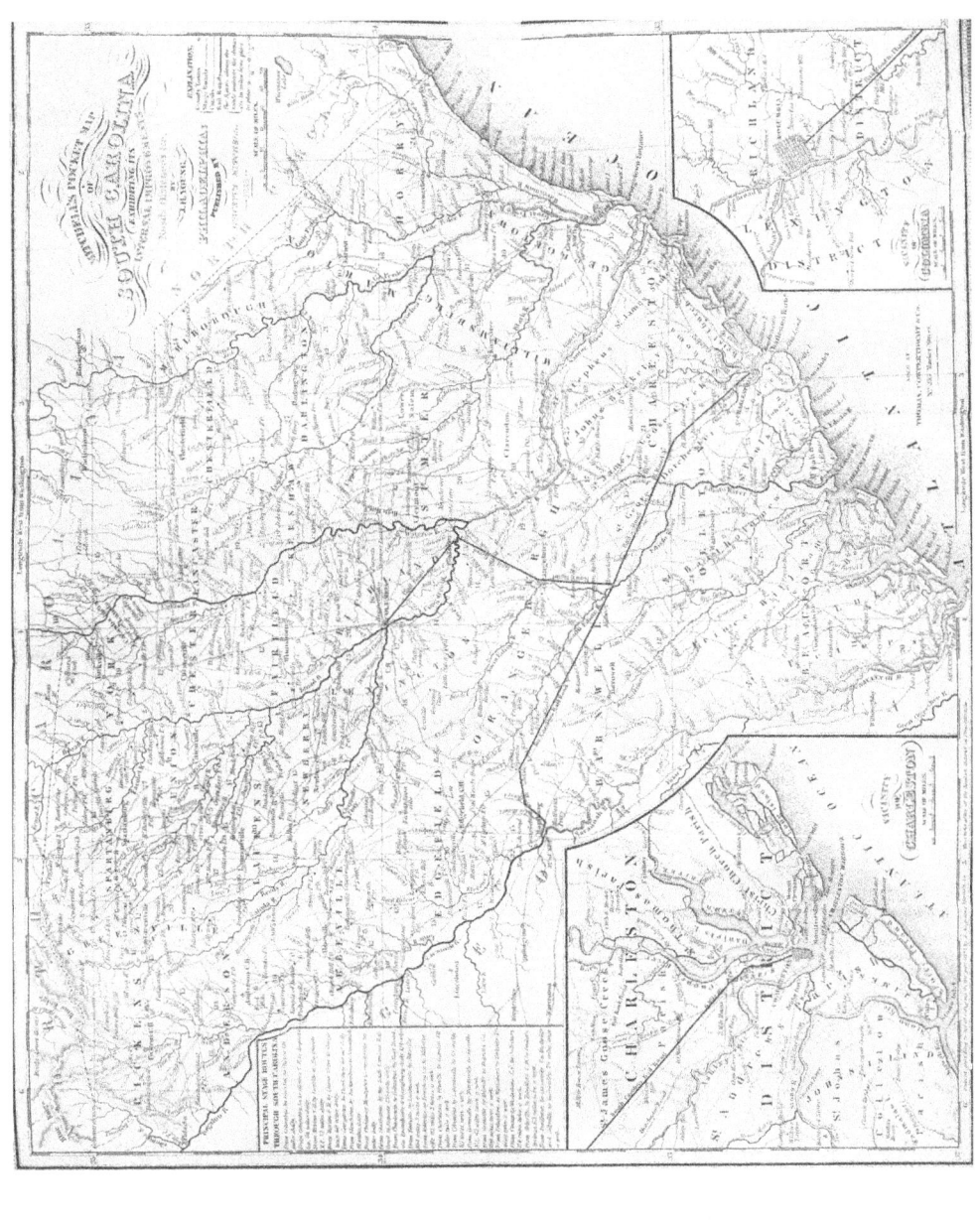

THE

GEOGRAPHY

OF

SOUTH CAROLINA:

BEING A COMPANION TO THE

HISTORY OF THAT STATE:

BY

WILLIAM GILMORE SIMMS.

COMPILED

FROM THE LATEST AND BEST AUTHORITIES,

AND DESIGNED FOR

THE INSTRUCTION OF THE YOUNG.

CHARLESTON.
PUBLISHED BY BABCOCK & CO.

1843.

ENTERED,
According to the Act of Congress, in the year 1843,
By William Gilmore Simms,
In the Office of the Clerk of the District Court of
SOUTH CAROLINA.

PREFACE.

This work is designed as a sequel, or companion, to my History of the State of South Carolina. In separating the political and social from the geographical history of the state, the object was to simplify the subject, and so to preserve unbroken the stream of narrative in the former work, as to make its perusal by the youthful reader, a pleasure rather than a task. A publication more immediately contemplating the statistical resources and physical character of the country, seems necessary in every point of view, as well to the student as the citizen. This publication, it is hoped, will meet the requisitions of the two. The materials for such a work are very copious. Perhaps no state in the Union has been more accurately surveyed, or is so excellently illustrated by maps. The liberality of the legislature, which has contributed largely to the latter, and the industry of Mr. Robert Mills, whose elaborate work on the statistics of the state has been freely made use of by the writer of this, have left us no reason to complain of any deficiencies. Indeed, the only difficulty in the preparation of such a compend as the following, is to know what portions will best bear contraction, and in what respects omissions will be least detrimental to the value of the work. The late census of the state, taken by the local authorities, enables us to speak with more elaborate certainty on the subject of the several district statistics, their population, pursuits and products; and the greatly increased energies of the agricultural departments provides us with additional facts and suggestions, which must prove of equal and important interest to the learner and inquirer.

I take leave to inscribe this little volume

TO

SOUTHERN TEACHERS:

MANY OF WHOM HAVE LONG FELT THE WANT OF SUITABLE

BOOKS FOR THE EDUCATION OF SOUTHERN CHILDREN;

ALL OF WHOM MUST FEEL THE EQUALLY SERIOUS NECESSITY OF HAVING SUCH

BOOKS PREPARED BY SOUTHERN MEN,

ACQUAINTED WITH OUR MANNERS AND CHARACTERISTICS—IDENTIFIED

WITH OUR INTERESTS—AND SPEAKING, AT THE SAME TIME,

THE LANGUAGE OF PATRIOTISM AND TRUTH.

THE AUTHOR.

CONTENTS.

SOUTH CAROLINA.

	Page
Situation, boundaries and extent,	9
Mountains and rivers,	10
Natural History,	12
Fruit and forest trees, birds, fish, &c.	12
Physical features,	14
Aborigines,	15
Population,	16
Government,	16
Chief cities, towns, and villages,	17
Education, public and private,	17
Morals, manners and religion,	18
Public works and buildings,	19
Revenue and resources,	20
Penal code,	20
Agriculture, commerce and manufactures,	21
Commerce,	22
General summary,—Civil and military history,	23
Districts, divisions,	28
Abbeville District,	30
Barnwell, "	34
Beaufort, "	38
Charleston, "	43
City of Charleston,	49
Domestic exports of South Carolina from 1819 to 1841,	56
Chester District,	58
Chesterfield "	61
Colleton "	64
Darlington "	69
Edgefield "	72

CONTENTS.

	Page
Fairfield District,	76
Georgetown "	80
Greenville "	83
Horry "	86
Kershaw "	88
Lancaster, "	91
Laurens, "	95
Lexington "	98
Marion "	102
Marlborough "	104
Newberry "	108
Orangeburg "	112
Pendleton, " (Pickens and Anderson,)	116
Richland, "	122
Spartanburg "	128
Sumter, "	132
Union "	136
Williamsburg "	140
York "	143

APPENDIX.

Aggregate population of the state,	147
Aggregate statistics of the state, June 1, 1840,	151
Statistics of the early Agriculture and Commerce,	169
Additions and corrections,	173
Questions,	177

NOTE.—ERRATA.

For the correction of sundry errors, the reader and student will please refer to the Appendix, pp. 173—175. Some of these corrections relate to the district boundaries, and are accordingly of vital importance. In a future edition, these errors,—the natural result of the author's distance from the press,—will receive correction in the proper place.

THE GEOGRAPHY

OF THE

STATE OF SOUTH CAROLINA.

SOUTH CAROLINA.

SITUATION, BOUNDARIES AND EXTENT.

SOUTH CAROLINA, one of the United States, is bounded, north by North Carolina; east by the Atlantic ocean; south-west and west, by the state of Georgia. Its average length is nearly two hundred miles; its breadth one hundred and sixty. It contains 30,213 square miles, or nearly 20,000,000 of acres. The soil of this territory has been divided into six classes, viz:—tide swamp, inland swamp, high river swamp, salt marsh, oak and hickory land, and pine barren. The first two classes are adapted to the culture of rice and hemp; the third and fifth to the growth of corn, hemp and indigo; the fourth, or salt marsh land, has been neglected; the pine barren is least productive of all, but possesses, with the oak and hickory land, the superior advantages of a salubrious climate. Without following a division so minute, it will be enough to say, that the territory of South Carolina presents an exceeding variety of soil and surface. Along the seaboard, and for forty miles into the interior, the face of the country is flat and unpromising; covered with extensive tracts of pine barren, swamp and savannah; comprising the most fertile and the most sterile extremes of soil. As you ascend towards the center of the state, the country rises into hills of moderate elevation. Advancing still farther, in a westerly direction, it becomes mountainous and very beautiful. The first section, which is generally called the lower country, includes the sea-islands, which are famous for the growth of the finest kinds of cotton, to which they impart their name; and the tide-lands, which are equally famous for their valuable crops of rice. The high lands of this region are generally poor,—only occasionally laced by thin little stripes of great fertility. The climate is moist, very changeable, and, during the summer and autumn months, extremely unhealthy.

The region which lies between the tide lands and the granite, or mountain ridges, is called the middle country; is more uniform in its temperature than either the lower or upper sections; less healthy in summer than the latter, and much more so than the former. In winter and spring it may be regarded as much more healthy than either. All this region is well irrigated by rivers and water courses. It possesses, amidst long and barren tracts of swamp and forest, many choice spots for culture, and yields, in tolerable abundance, the kind of cotton which is called upland or short staple. The productions of the state are very generally the same. In addition to cotton and rice, which are chiefly the products of the lower and middle sections, there is a numerous list of commodities, which show a happy variety in the resources of the country. These consist of corn and potatoes; wheat, peas, rye and oats; tobacco and indigo; lumber, tar, pitch and turpentine; oils and silks, and many other products, in varying quantity and differing value. Among the metals and minerals found in the state, are gold, iron and lead; plumbago, pyrites, asbestos; granite, oil and soap stones, and many others.

MOUNTAINS AND RIVERS.

A few spurs from the great range of the Blue Ridge mountains, penetrate the north west corner of South Carolina. The most extensive of these is the Saluda mountain, which forms the northwest boundary line of the state. Detached and prominent spurs project from this mountain, and under the several names of Table mountain, Oconee, Estatoee, Sassafras, Oolenoee, Paris and King's mountain, present conspicuous objects of survey in the districts which they occupy. The scenery of this region is particularly beautiful ;—a pleasing variety of rock, valley, cascade and cultivated plain, renders it a favorite resort for the summer traveler ; while its bracing air and salubrious climate, make it equally attractive to the invalid seeking health in a purer atmosphere.

The rivers in South Carolina are numerous, and will be found hereafter much more valuable than they have heretofore proved. The principal are, the Savannah, which divides South Carolina from Georgia ; the Congaree, the Santee, Wateree, Catawba, Saluda, Pedee, Edisto and Waccamaw. Among the smaller streams are the Wenee, (Black,) Eswapuddenah, (Broad,) Amoyeschek, (Tyger,) Enoree, Kaddipah, (Lynch,) Combahee, Salkehatchie, (Saltcatcher,) Pocotaligo, Pacolet, Ashepoo, Stono, Wando and Tugaloo. The Keawah, (Ashley,) and Etiwan, (Cooper,) are rather arms of the sea than mere rivers, and unite in forming the basin and harbor of Charleston. Numerous smaller streams, creeks and inlets, which are called rivers, traverse the Atlantic coast along the south-east border of the state, and afford many convenient places of access from the sea ;—bays and harbors, which are landlocked by the numerous islands among which they lie. The peculiarity of the rivers in South Carolina, which distinguishes them from those of the north, is the considerable bodies of alluvial soil which line their margins, enlarging as they descend, so as, in the main rivers, to be in some places several miles wide. These borders are immensely fertile, and when reclaimed, far surpass the powers of production in most other soils. In some instances, two thousand pounds of cotton in the seed, have been raised, in these reclaimed tracts, to the acre.

NATURAL HISTORY.

CLIMATE.—The climate of South Carolina, though subject to some considerable fluctuations within the few last years, is yet very much like that of the West Indies. Six or seven months in the year pass without frost. The cold is seldom intense. The period of vegetation comprehends seven or eight months. The fruits which mature and flourish, are figs, apricots, cherries, nectarines, apples, peaches, pears, melons and pomegranates.— Oranges are uninjured in ordinary winters. Olives, almonds, pechan nuts, and the sugar cane, succeed in the lower parts of the state. To these may be added, as fruits of natural and easy growth, blackberries, strawberries and raspberries; plums and whortleberries, grapes, chestnuts, chinquapins and persimmons. Among the esculent vegetables, which are raised with common diligence, are English peas, asparagus, green corn, the squash, okra, tomato, artichoke, potato and cabbage; beans of all kinds; beets, carrots and cucumbers.

The atmospherical phenomena to which South Carolina is subject, are equally terrible and splendid. Thunder storms are frequent during the summer months; the lightning is close, keen and frequently destructive of life. The thunder, during the same period, is a prolonged, repeated, and most stunning explosion. In 1775, the city of Charleston was visited by one of these storms, in which there were five houses, as many ships, and two churches, struck by lightning. Earthquakes have been felt, but are not frequent. They have never been attended with danger in South Carolina. But the hurricane and the whirlwind, to which the climate is also subject, have not been equally harmless.

FRUIT AND FOREST TREES, BIRDS, FISH, &C.

The botanical wealth of South Carolina is very great. She is rich in native and exotic productions; plants of rare and medicinal qualities; fruits of the most luscious description; shrubs, vines and flowers, of exquisite beauty, fragrance and variety, and forest trees of the noblest growth and value. Among these may be enumerated, the numerous varieties of the oak, the laurel, the ash, the hickory, the gum, the holly, the beech, the cypress, elm, pine, maple, poplar, walnut, bay, sycamore and palmetto. But these form but a small part of the long and various catalogue.

The animals, native to the state, are the mammoth, the buffalo, catamount and beaver, (all now extinct.) The bear, the panther, wild cat, wolf, red fox, red deer, otter, moose, squirrel, (gray, black, red, ground, and flying,) rabbit, pole-cat, mole, mink, opossum, raccoon, lizard, toad, frog, muskrat and weazel.

The birds are very numerous, and include the following: the eagle, hawk, turkey, owl, cormorant, crane, curlew, goose, buzzard, crow, wood-pecker, titmouse, creeper, humming-bird, cuckoo, paroquet, jay, jackdaw, starling, rice-bird, mocking-bird, nuthatch, pigeon, dove, robin, thrush, bulfinch, duck, grosbeak, gannet, sparrow, snow-bird, finch, nonpareil, linnet, kingfisher, plover, heron, bittern, Indian pullet, sanguillah, pelican, pheasant, partridge, wren, swallow, marten, chatterer, flycatcher, blue-bird, red-bird, titmouse, goat-sucker, or chuck-will's widow, or Carolina whippoorwill; snipe, woodcock, marsh-hen and flamingo. Of many of these birds there are several varieties. Some of them, as the goose, some species of the duck, the pigeon, snow-bird and a few others, are birds of passage, which visit us only at certain times of the year.

The salt water fish are, the shark, the porpoise, drum, bass, cavalli, sheep's head, shad, whiting, porgy, blackfish, mullet, herring, skip-Jack, sailor's choice, crocus, sole, angel-fish, yellow tail, alewife, &c.

Those which inhabit fresh waters are, pike, sturgeon, trout, bream, rock, mud, perch, suck, cat, gar, soft shelled turtle, terrapin, &c.

Of the shell fish, there are several kinds of large and small sea turtle, oysters, crabs, shrimps, clams and muscles.

The reptiles are the rattlesnake, viper, copper belly, hognose, wampum, horn, thunder, black, chain, glass, ribbon, moccasin, coach whip, green and bull snakes. The bite of some of these is fatal. There are many others which may be added to the list.

The insects are numerous;—many kinds of worm—the snail, the bug, flea, forty legs, cicada, woodlouse, cricket, cockroach, beetle, glow-worm, firefly, butterfly, moth, ant, fig-eater, bee, wasp, hornet, honey-bee, fly, spider, sandfly, tick and musquito.

PHYSICAL FEATURES.

One half of South Carolina is supposed to be of alluvial formation. The other half primitive. The alluvial extends about one hundred miles from the sea coast.— The primitive occupies the residue. The proofs of the formation of the first division are abundant. The marine shell, limestone, and its attendants, are every where seen. The upper boundary of this region is at Shell bluff, on Savannah river, in Barnwell district. From thence it crosses the state in a nearly direct line, passing through the upper edge of Marion district into North Carolina. Within the primitive formation is found the granite with its attendants. The lower boundary of this region begins just above Hamburg, on the Savannah river, passes a little below Columbia, one mile above Camden, a little above Cheraw, and enters North Carolina near Fayetteville. The whole lower country of South Carolina was once probably covered by the ocean. The cuts made across peninsulas near the sea coast, have laid bare whole forests of subterraneous cypress timber. Marine shells of great size are found sixty miles from the ocean, at a depth of seven feet from the surface, in immense quarries, and in a regular vein, or track, which extends to the Oconee river in Georgia. No primitive stones or rocks are found within one hundred miles from the sea. Such as occur are of the shell limestone species, with occasional sandstone. These, near the junction of the rivers Congaree and Wateree, are mixed with a portion of iron ore. The face of the lower country is so uniform and level, that the traveler is conscious of no rise, until he approaches the sand hills, about fifty or sixty miles from the coast, where he finds a considerable rapid ascent, in the distance of a single mile, of two or three hundred feet. The country then becomes broken, and so continues, with occasional intervals of plain, until we reach the foot of the mountains. Here some considerable masses from the Alleghany ridge project into the state, the summits of which rise, as in the case of the Table mountain, nearly four thousand feet above the sea. The scenery of this region is equally various and sublime. The eye never tires of a prospect which is constantly changing. The mountains which lie between the Chatuga and the Estatoe, are lofty, narrow ridges, covered with shrubs and trees, with deep valleys between—rocky gorges almost totally unfit for cultivation. In these gorges are numerous crystal torrents, and from the mountains are small cascades, and along the fragmentary rocks, shallow rivers brawl along in constant foam and impatience. The stupendous precipice called the Table mountain, is an object of great curiosity and admiration. It is a naked rock of granite, almost perpendicular on three sides, eleven hundred feet from its base. The waters trickling down its sides have worn numerous channels, which give its surface a fluted appearance. When the sun strikes upon these trickling waters, they seem so many showers of brilliants. From this eminence the prospect is equally grand and extensive. From one point of view, you can see five cascades, of unequal size, at a single glance of the eye.

ABORIGINES.

South Carolina, at the coming of the European settlers, was occupied by no less than twenty-eight nations or tribes of Indians. The chief of these were the Chickasaw, the Cherokee, Catawba, Muscoghee and Choctaw. The inferior were the Yemassee, Congaree, Santee, Wateree, Saluda, Chickaree and Serratee.— These, with the exception of the Catawba, are either extinct, or have emigrated to the south-west. Of the

Catawba, but a miserable and profligate few remain ; delivered up to the basest indolence, and the most wretched drunkenness. The Indian names, which have been numerously preserved throughout the state, will show, in most respects, the regions which they severally occupied ; as the Congarees occupied the country which is watered by the river of that name ; the Santees, the Santee ; the Saludahs, the Saluda ; and so on, with the Wateree, the Pedee, the Edisto, and many others.

POPULATION.

The population of the state of South Carolina, by the census of 1840, makes a total of 594,439 inhabitants.— Of these, 259,002 are white ; 8,279 free colored, and 327,158 slaves. Of this number, 200,000 are computed to be engaged in agriculture ; 2000 in commerce ; 10,000 in trades and manufactures ; 500 in the navigation of the seas ; 500 in the navigation of canals, lakes and rivers, and 1500 in the liberal professions. It is probable that all these estimates are too low.

The militia force of the state consists of five divisions, comprising ten brigades and forty-six regiments, and numbers about 50,000 men, rank and file.

GOVERNMENT.

South Carolina is a representative democracy. The people are the sources of power. The right of suffrage belongs to all free white citizens not degraded by crime, and this principle secures the adoption of equal laws and moderate taxation. The government of the state, in its several departments, is entrusted to three bodies—namely, the Legislature, which makes the laws, the Judiciary by which they are expounded and interpreted, and the Executive, or Governor, by whom they are enforced.— The Legislature consists of two chambers; the one a Senate, the other, a House of Representatives. The senators are forty-five in number, and are elected for a term of four years. Each district or parish is entitled to a senator. The members of the House of Representatives are one hundred and twenty-four in number, and are elected for two years. A mixed basis of population and property determines the number of delegates which are allotted to the several districts.

The judicial power is vested in ten judges. The courts are three in number—Law, Equity and Appeal.— The two former are common to all the districts. The latter is held only at Charleston and Columbia.

The executive authority is confided to a Governor, and in the event of his death or incompetence, to a Lieutenant-Governor, who is elected at the same time with himself. The Governor, Lieutenant-Governor, Judges, Solicitors, Masters and Commissioners in Equity, and Treasurer of the State, are elected by the Legislature. The election of most other officers has been reserved to the people.

CHIEF CITIES, TOWNS AND VILLAGES.

Charleston is the metropolis of the state. It lies at the junction of the two rivers, Cooper and Ashley. It was founded in 1680. It has a population, (the suburbs or neck, included) of 41,000 inhabitants. (*See Charleston District.*) Columbia is the capital of the State. It lies on the east bank of the Congaree river.— (*see Richland District.*) Camden, (*see Kershaw District.*) Georgetown, Beaufort, Cheraw, (*see Chesterfield District.*) Hamburgh, (*see Edgefield District.*) Aiken, (*see Barnwell District.*) Walterborough, (*see Colleton District.*) Greenville, Pendleton, Edgefield and Coosawatchie, (*see Beaufort District.*) Sumterville, Statesburg, (*see Sumter District.*) Lancaster, Barnwell, Orangeburg, Abbeville, Yorkville, Spartanburg, Winnsboro', Summerville, and many others.

EDUCATION, PUBLIC AND PRIVATE.

The state of South Carolina has shown itself properly sensible to the necessity of public education in a country where the people govern. The College of the State, at

Columbia, was a liberal and fortunate endowment. It was established in 1802, and receives a large annual appropriation from the Legislature. It has sent forth some of the ablest men in the nation. It is now in a highly flourishing condition. The officers are a president, six professors, and two tutors. There is an annual appropriation of two thousand dollars for the library, which already contains several thousand volumes, well selected and excellently arranged in a building especially devoted to this object. An annual appropriation of near forty thousand dollars is made to the free or public schools throughout the state; but the results from this appropriation are less satisfactory than that to the college. The free school system is only partially successful.

The private institutions for educational purposes are numerous and valuable. The corporation of Charleston have beneficently endowed, and sustain with annual appropriations, a college and high school, which are well governed and are producing excellent results. The Medical College of South Carolina, in Charleston, is a highly flourishing school of science.

MORALS, MANNERS AND RELIGION.

The morals and manners of the South Carolinians, have always been regarded as among the best in the Union. The early settlers came from good stock at home, and, up to the time of the revolution, the young men of family were mostly sent to Europe for education. They are characterized by a nice sense of propriety and honor; a high, but not haughty carriage, and an equal ease and dignity of carriage and expression.— The religion of the state is mostly Protestant. The Catholics are not numerous, but respectable. They have in Charleston a Convent and a Theological Seminary. The Baptists have a Theological Seminary in Edgefield, the Lutherans in Newberry, and, in Columbia, the Synod of South Carolina and Georgia have one also. There are other schools and seminaries, of different persuasions, in exercise or contemplation, in various other parts of the state.

PUBLIC WORKS AND BUILDINGS.

The state has appropriated largely, and not always with success, to works of internal improvement. Several millions have been appropriated in this way, and much of it wasted. Still, something has been gained to the comfort of the people, if not to the resources of the country. Obstructions have been removed from rivers, canals have been dug, and shoals and falls overcome by industry and art. A great state road, passing from Charleston, by way of Columbia, through the Saluda Gap, facilitates communication with Buncombe, North Carolina. Numerous causeways, of great length, in various parts of the country, have overcome morasses which were otherwise impassable. The Santee Canal is twenty two miles in length, and a work of great difficulty, cost and importance. The Charleston and Hamburg Rail Road, was, at one time, the longest work of the kind in the world. It is one hundred and thirty-six miles in length. This road passes from Charleston to Summerville, (22 miles,) to Branchville, (62,) crosses the Edisto to Midway, (72,) to Grahamville, (81,) to Blackville, (90,) to Williston, (100,) to Aiken, (120,) and Hamburg, (136.) From Branchville, it extends an arm to Columbia, passing by the village of Orangeburg, which is 80 miles from Charleston, from thence to Lewisville, (92,) thence across the Congaree river, to Gadsden, (111,) and on to Columbia, a distance from Charleston of 131 miles.

The public buildings of the state are numerous, generally of durable materials and tasteful architecture.— Among these is the Lunatic Asylum in Columbia,—a building imposing in externals, very spacious, and proof against fire. It is large enough to accommodate one hundred and twenty patients, besides having large corridors, hospitals, refectories, parlors, keepers' apartments, sundry offices, kitchens, and a medical hall. The cost of this structure approaches $100,000. The State House, or House of Assembly, is a far less valuable and imposing structure; built of wood, according to a plan, mean, ineligible and obscure. It is something of a reproach to the state, that, while making large annual appropriations for other objects, a nobler fabric should not be substituted for this. The college buildings, also in Columbia, are good, solid and spacious fabrics. The library lately built, is an architectural improvement upon former plans. In Charleston there are several excellent buildings belonging to the state. Such are the Court House, the fire proof building in which the archives and public offices are kept, and the banking house of the state fiscal institution.

REVENUE AND RESOURCES.

The revenue of the state is chiefly derived from assessments on lands, negroes, city and town lots, stock in trade, dividends from the Bank of the State, &c. The ordinary revenue from these sources, is about four hundred thousand dollars, and the expenses of the state are so regulated as ordinarily to fall within this sum. The debt of the state, at this time, may be set down as about five millions. The fiscal department is under the management of a Comptroller General. There are two State Treasurers, one for the upper and one for the lower division of the state.

THE PENAL CODE

Of South Carolina, with sundry modifications, is that of Great Britain. The common law of England has been declared by statute, to be of force, except in certain enumerated cases. All the statutes of England, which guarantee the right and liberties of the subject, are of force in South Carolina. The criminal laws, though milder in character than those of Great Britain, and perhaps less rigidly administered, are yet supposed to need farther modification. A nicer discrimination between offences and the proper degrees of punishment, seems to be necessary; and the tendency of public opinion begins to incline towards the adoption of the penitentiary system, as a grand agent in the proper regulation of this subject; particularly in bringing about the substitution of solitary confinement for life, in lieu of the punishment of death.

AGRICULTURE, COMMERCE AND MANUFACTURES.

The statistical returns of 1840, give 200,000 persons as the number employed in agriculture in South Carolina. This is probably much below the true number. We are of opinion, that two thirds of the state are thus employed, in one or other of the departments of rural industry. In the lower districts, the labors of the field are chiefly performed by slaves. The proportion of whites to blacks is, therefore, comparatively small in several of these districts. In the middle country, the population is very equally composed of white and black. In the upper districts, the proportion is greatly in favor of the former. The slaves are very prolific, increasing in greater proportion than the whites; a sufficient proof of the mildness of their servitude and labor. The agricultural industry of the country, though resulting in temporary success, chiefly from the newness and great fertility of the soil, has been of that injurious kind which has tended very much to its exhaustion. It is only of late years that manure has been employed, and it is not even yet made use of generally. The improvement in this and other respects, though gradual, is certain. Agricultural societies are active, and usefully engaged in all the districts, under the direction of able and influential men. The State Agricultural Society, which meets annually at Columbia, holds a cattle fair and distributes premiums, has given a decided impulse to the popular mind on this important subject. The staples of Carolina have been indigo, tobacco, rice, and cotton. The two former are now very little cultivated. Her exports beside, have been tar, turpentine, lumber, peltry, &c. These latter articles were, during the proprietary government, her only exports. Rice was introduced in 1690 from Madagascar, and in 1841, the export of this article reached 110,000 barrels. Indigo was introduced in 1741 from Antigua, and at the beginning of the revolution, the export of this article was 1,200,000 pounds. The first cultivation of tobacco was introduced sometime prior to the revolution, and probably superseded and led to the final abandonment of indigo as a staple. It was cultivated with profit for twenty years after the war with England. Cotton was cultivated as a curiosity in South Carolina, as early as 1720, but was adopted slowly into the general cultivation. In 1795, the export was about 3,500 bales. In 1839, it was 300,000 bales.

The vine, the olive, and the silk worm, are interests to which the people of South Carolina have never done justice. It is not improbable that one or other, or all of these commodities, will be resorted to, in the comparative decline of value in the present staple, cotton. There are numerous other articles beside these, which would reward cultivation in Carolina. The country is fine for grazing, and a better attention to stock, horses and sheep, will amply recompense the planter for any diminution in the value of the great staples.

Indian corn, or maize, is cultivated with tolerable success. The production of wheat is increasing. Silk, of which South Carolina exported ten thousand pounds so far back as 1760, is produced in some of the middle districts, and may be increased in all. If ever there was a country more particularly designed than any other for the raising of the mulberry and the silk worm, it is the pine barrens of South Carolina. For the official returns of the state census of 1840, which includes a classification and summary of its stock, produce, &c. *See Appendix.*

COMMERCE.

The commerce of South Carolina is not now in her own hands. Her produce is unhappily almost entirely carried off by foreign shipping. In this particular, she has not maintained her position. Her native commerce was once very extensive. Some of her first families distinguished themselves in the foreign trade, and rendered it honorable at home. Some late efforts have been making to regain this position, and she now boasts of a few very fine and prosperous ships, which ply between Charleston, Liverpool, London, and Havre. The commercial houses of South Carolina, engaged in foreign trade, are set down at thirty; a number, it is thought, rather too low. The commission houses are forty-one; retail dry good and other stores, twelve hundred and sixty-two. Lumber yards and trade, seventeen. The capital invested in these several departments, is estimated at ten and a half millions of dollars; the persons employed in them, are numbered at twelve to fifteen hundred.—[*See Charleston District.*]

GENERAL SUMMARY.

CIVIL AND MILITARY HISTORY.

1497.] South Carolina is first discovered in 1497, by Sebastian Cabot. Her territory is claimed by France, England, and Spain, either by right of conquest, purchase, or discovery; but no settlement is effected upon the soil for nearly seventy years.

1520.] Lucas Vasquez de Ayllon, with two slave ships, enters the Combahee river, and carries two hundred of the natives of Chickora—as that part of Carolina was then called by the aborigines—into captivity. One of these ships, with all her captives and crew, perishes at sea.

1525.] Lucas Vasquez de Ayllon returns this year, with a large fleet, a second time to the river Combahee. His largest ship founders in that river; his people set upon by the natives and massacred. His own fate doubtful.

1562.] In this year, France sends out a colony of Protestant Christians, who settle on or about Port Royal island, in the harbor of that name. This colony gives names to the rivers, Broad, May, and Port Royal. Oppressed by privation and mutiny, the company abandons the settlement in the following year, and returns to France.

1564.] A second colony of French Protestants arrives, but, discouraged by the late of the first, they settle at a station to the south of it, the precise location being doubtful. This settlement is destroyed by the Spaniards, and the Frenchmen cruelly murdered.

1670.] No permanent settlement of Carolina, by Europeans, takes place until 1670, when a small body of English emigrants, under William Sayle, arrives at Port Royal island. Hence they remove [1671] to Ashley river, where they establish old Charlestown. From this spot they again remove, in 1679, to the tongue of land called Oyster Point, formed by the confluence of the rivers Keawah and Etiwan, now known as Ashley and Cooper, where they founded the present city of Charleston.

1680.] The first Indian war takes place, which nearly ruins the colony.

1682.] A colony from Scotland, under lord Cardross, settles at Port Royal.

1686.] The settlers at Port Royal dislodged and dispersed by a body of Spaniards from St. Augustine.

1690.] Popular discontents with the proprietary government.

1702.] Governor Moore undertakes a military expedition against the Spaniards of Florida.

1703.] War with the Apalachian Indians.

1706.] The French and Spaniards make a combined attack on Charleston and are defeated.

———.] Colonel Palmer, of South Carolina, with three hundred men, makes a successful incursion into Florida.

1710.] The Free School system first established.

1712.] A dangerous conspiracy of the North Carolina Indians, defeated by colonel Barnwell.

1715.] The Yemassee war, which threatens the destruction of the colony; the Indians defeated by governor Craven.

1720.] The proprietary government thrown off; that of the crown established.

1728.] Wars with the pirates, who are destroyed. A dreadful hurricane; the tide overflows Charleston.

1740.] Charleston half destroyed by fire.

1741.] Indigo first planted.

1752.] A dreadful hurricane.

1760.] Camden laid out.

1769.] South Carolina divided into seven precincts, viz:—Charleston, Georgetown, Beaufort, Orangeburg, Cheraw, Camden, and Ninety-Six.

1774.] First act passed to oppose royal usurpation by force.

1775.] Prohibition to import British goods. The people enter into association for the defence of their rights. First military force raised for defence of the colony against the crown.

1776.] Battle of Fort Moultrie, and defeat of the British fleet.

———.] Constitution framed—the first of the union.

———.] Indians and tories defeated in the interior.

1777–8.] South Carolina enjoys a lucrative commerce.

1779.] The British defeated at Port Royal by general Moultrie.

———.] Col. Pickens defeats the British and tories.

1779] Charleston beleaguered by general Provost—summoned—refuses to surrender. Provost retires on the approach of general Lincoln.

———.] Battle of Stono, between Lincoln and Provost. A French force under count D'Estaing, with the American under Lincoln, assault Savannah and are defeated.

1780.] Charleston besieged by sir Henry Clinton—is taken after a leaguer of six weeks. Fort Motte taken by general Marion. Battle of Camden between general Gates and lord Cornwallis; the former defeated with great loss. Colonel Williams defeats the British at Musgroves' mill. Sumter defeated at Fishing creek by Tarleton. General Marion is victorious in several battles with the tories. Battle at King's mountain—the British under colonel Ferguson defeated with great loss. Sumter gains several victories over the British and tories at Broad river and Blackstock's.

1781.] Battle of the Cowpens; Morgan defeats Tarleton with great loss. Frequent victories of the partizans, Sumter, Marion, Taylor, Harden and others, over the British and tories. The American cavalry surprized and routed at Monk's corner by Tarleton.

———.] General Marion, with colonel Lee, takes Fort Watson. Battle of Hobkirk's Hill. Lord Rawdon evacuates Camden. General Greene besieges the British post at Ninety-Six; assaults it; raises the siege on the approach of Rawdon. Greene offers battle to Rawdon at Orangeburg; he declines. Captain Eggleston captures the British horse near the Saluda. General Sumter expels the British garrison from Biggins' church. Colonel Isaac Hayne captured and executed by the British. Battle of the Eutaws; the British defeated with great loss. General Pickens invades the Cherokee country, conquers and makes them sue for peace. Greene surprises the British at Dorchester.

1782.] General Gist attacks the British force at Combahee ferry; Colonel Laurens slain. The British evacuate Charleston.

1783.] Charleston incorporated.

1785.] The Methodists first establish themselves as a church.

1786.] Columbia founded as the seat of government, and laid out as a town.

1790.] The present constitution of the State ratified at Columbia, June 3.

1791.] Right of primogeniture abolished. The Roman Catholics first establish themselves as a church. General Washington visits South Carolina.

1792.] Orphan House established in Charleston.

1794.] Cotton first exported.

1798.] The state divided into twenty-four districts, counties and parishes; and subsequently into the present number, twenty-eight districts.

1800.] County courts abolished; district courts established in the several districts.

1804.] Dreadful hurricane, which destroys a vast amount of property.

1807.] Right of suffrage extended to all citizens.

1811.] Establishment of general free school system.

1812.] Bank of the State created.

1821.] Hamburg founded.

1822.] Destructive hurricane, with loss of life, in the low country. Insurrection among the negroes of Charleston discovered, defeated and punished.

1824.] The courts of law new modelled. General Lafayette revisits Carolina.

1827.] Legislature of South Carolina passes resolutions against the protective tariff of the United States, as unconstitutional.

1830.] South Carolina enacts an ordinance to declare null and void an act of Congress, imposing duties, &c.

1833.] Counter proclamations of president Jackson and governor Hayne, on the subject of nullification.

1839.] State Agricultural Society established.

1840.] Governor Noble dies; is succeeded by lieutenant-governor Henegan.

———.] John P. Richardson of Sumter, elected, governor.

1842.] James H. Hammond, of Barnwell, nominated as governor: ——— ———, lieutenant-governor.

DISTRICTS, DIVISIONS.

South Carolina is divided into twenty-eight districts, namely,—

1, Abbeville,	11, Georgetown,	20, Newberry,
2, Barnwell,	12, Greenville,	21, Orangeburg,
3, Beaufort,	13, Horry,	22, Pendleton,
4, Charleston,	14, Kershaw,	23, Richland,
5, Chester,	15, Lancaster,	24, Spartanburg,
6, Chesterfield,	16. Laurens,	25, Sumter,
7, Colleton,	17. Lexington,	26, Union,
8, Darlington,	18, Marion,	27, Williamsburg
9, Edgefield,	19, Marlborough	28, York.
10, Fairfield,		

One of these districts, Pendleton, is again divided, for judicial purposes only, into two other districts, namely,—Anderson and Pickens. There is yet a minuter division of certain of the districts into parishes, with the view to convenience, and a more easy and equal distribution of political power of the state. The districts so divided, are Charleston, Colleton, Beaufort, Orangeburg and Georgetown. Charleston, contains ten parishes, namely,—St. Andrew, Christ's Church, St. James, (Goose creek,) St. James, (Santee,) St. John, (Berkley,) St. John, (Colleton,) St. Michael, and St. Philip, (these form the city and suburbs of Charleston, St. Stephen and St. Thomas. These parishes are independent divisions, which elect their own members, and regulate themselves by distinct municipal laws.

Colleton contains three parishes, namely,—St. Bartholomew, St. George, and St. Paul.

Beaufort contains four parishes, namely,—St. Helena, St. Luke, St. Peter, and Prince William.

Georgetown comprises the two parishes of All-Saints and Prince George, (Winyaw.)

Orangeburg is subdivided into the two parishes of St. Matthew and Orange.

All of these parishional divisions were originally those of church government. They are continued now for political convenience. The parishes are twenty-one in number.

The congressional districts of South Carolina, according to the present representative ratio, are nine in number, viz—.1. The district of Charleston. 2. The districts of Colleton and Beaufort. 3. The districts of Georgetown, Horry, Marion, Marlborough, Williamsburgh, and Darlington. 4. The districts of Barnwell, Orangeburg, Lexington, and Richland. 5. Edgefield and Abbeville. 6. Pendleton and Greenville. 7. Spartanburg, Union, York, and Chester. 8. Lancaster, Kershaw, Sumter, and Chesterfield. 9. Fairfield, Newberry, and Laurens.

A new apportionment of the congressional districts will be required under an act of Congress, by which the representation of South Carolina will be reduced from nine to seven members.

ABBEVILLE DISTRICT.

ABBEVILLE DISTRICT is bounded on the south-west by the Savannah river, on the north-east by the Saluda, on the south-east by Edgefield district, and on the north-west by Pendleton. It lies within the granite region.—The soil is most generally clay, covered with a rich mould, and sometimes mixed with sand and gravel. The length of the district is thirty-two miles; breadth, thirty-one; and comprises 634,880 square acres. The climate is mild and agreeable throughout the year, and resembles, in some degree, that of the south of France. The silk worm was cultivated at one period with great success in this district, but has yielded to the greater profitableness of cotton. The diseases are not acute; the instances of extreme old age are numerous. Cotton is the principal market production; but corn, wheat, barley, hay, tobacco, wool, and a profitable and useful variety of other articles are raised, in considerable quantities. [*See return of Census for* 1840.] This district is well calculated for farming, and by a good manuring system, which is now very much adopted, the soil will be nourished and improved. The face of the country is hilly and picturesque. The lands are broken and undulating; in places abrupt and precipitous. There is an abundance of granite in the district; freestone, and a quarry of the species of oil or Turkey stone, has been worked to advantage. The timber trees are of a fine and noble growth, consisting of oaks, (the white, red and Spanish,) chesnut and poplar, black walnut, curled maple, wild cherry, hickory, dogwood, and many others. The pine is scarce and inferior. The fruit trees are the peach, apple, quince, cherry and plum; grapes, chesnuts, mulberries, &c.

The water courses are numerous and important.—Bounded on two sides by navigable rivers, Abbeville is intersected by several smaller streams, which furnish water at all seasons, manufacturing and mill seats in abundance, and a good variety of fish. Among these are the Sapona, the Seraw, and Rocky river besides many others of equal importance. It is to be regretted that so few of the Indian names of streams and places are preserved. In place of them we have such names as Hard-Labor, Broad-Mouth, and Cuffy-Town, which scarcely do justice to the pleasant and useful creeks and water courses, with which they are coupled. This district was originally a part of the great inheritance of the Cherokees. Game is scarce, as well birds as beasts; the necessary effect of a rapid increase of population. In 1800, the population of this district was 13,500. In 1840, it is 29,329. It is entitled to one senator and five representatives in the state Legislature.

Abbeville is the chief town. It is the seat of justice, in the center of the district, is pleasantly situated, two hundred miles from Charleston and eighty from Columbia, and contains five hundred inhabitants. It is well laid out; contains, besides the court house and jail, an arsenal and magazine, and about fifty dwelling houses. The buildings are good, and the town is laid out with neatness. There are several other towns, such as Cokesbury, a flourishing place of near 300 inhabitants, and Greenwood, which is also a thriving village. Vienna, Hampton and Willington, are generally unprosperous, in decay, and of little note. The village of Cambridge, containing a few houses, stores and taverns, is only remarkable as being upon or near the site of one of the most conspicuous of our country settlements before and during the war of the revolution. Here stood the fortress and village of Ninety-Six, in the district then of the same name,—a name derived from the distance which it bore to the frontier fort of Prince George. It stands in the eastern quarter of Abbeville, near the borders of Edgefield, and within six miles of the Saluda river. The village was one of size and considerable importance. The fortress, a portion of the ruins of which are still to be seen, was one which overawed the neighborhood on every hand, and through this influence became a recruiting fort for the British during the war, in which they accumulated levies in great numbers from among the tories, and from which they sent forth, night and day, their predatory bands for plunder and rapine. There was no portion of the state which suffered so much during the war, as this district. No one place that became of more importance to the success of either party in the interior. At length it was beleaguered by general Greene. The American mine is still to be traced, and may be followed for near thirty yards. The place was relieved by general Rawdon; but after a brief interval, was abandoned by the British. Soon after this evacuation, the fort of Ninety-Six and the surrounding country were suddenly invaded by the Cherokee Indians. These were chastised by general Pickens, who gathered the militia, defeated and drove the savages, pursued them into their own country, and retaliated upon them by the burning of fourteen of their towns, killing many of their warriors, and taking a greater number captive. A banditti of tories, disguised as Indians, about the same time made a similar fray into the district, and from these cruel circumstances, Cambridge seems never to have recovered, It is sparsely settled, but still possesses the attractions of a noble site, commanding elevation, agreeable scenery, and the traditions of past events of great interest and importance. It has been proposed to erect a monument on the spot, in honor of the patriotic deeds by which it is distinguished.

The first settlement in Abbeville was made in 1756. Two hundred French emigrants followed in 1764, and from these the district is supposed to have received its name, after a town in France. The inhabitants are Presbyterians, Methodists, Baptists and Episcopalians. The first sect is the most numerous, and exercised at an early period, a considerable influence in the educational establishments of the district. Abbeville was the place of education for a great portion of the upper country, until Columbia rose into her present important position as a central seat of learning.

The Clarke and Erskine Seminary, at Due West Corner, in this district, is a new and promising institution; the first commencement of which took place in Sept. 1842, with high credit to the faculty and pupils.

Abbeville has produced several eminent men, who have done honor to the whole country. Patrick Calhoun was a man of strong intellect and influence, and has been styled the patriarch of the district. General Pickens was one of our most successful partisan warriors; general Robert Anderson was another. Their names are written on many a battle field of Carolina. Colonel Williams, who fell at King's mountain, was also a native of this district; and the list besides, of dead and living persons, natives of Abbeville, who have become famous in our history, is unusually large.

BARNWELL DISTRICT.

BARNWELL is bounded on the north and north-east by Orangeburg; on the south-east by Beaufort and Colleton; on the south-west by the Savannah river; on the west by Edgefield. It is forty-eight miles in length, thirty in breadth, and contains 921,600 acres. The soil is light and sandy, bottomed on clay; the rich lands border the creeks and rivers. Portions of them are very fertile. The productions are cotton, lumber, corn, wheat, potatoes, rye, &c.

The face of the country is generally level; occasionally broken by gentle hills, and interspersed with numerous ponds, in which the waters are always limpid, supposed to be supplied by secret springs from below. Many of these ponds, having become filled up in the progress of years, present the appearance of so many natural meadows, not unlike the prairies of the west. This district lies below the granite region, and has none of that rock, unless in its extreme north-west angle, where it slightly dips into the primitive formation. Freestone abounds on the Edisto. Shell limestone is also found in considerable quantity.

The timber trees are oak, hickory, pine, cypress, poplar, ash, gum, cedar, dogwood, sassafras, &c. The pine forests are unusually extensive in the high lands, and the cypress in the swamps. The fruit trees are the apple, peach, pear, plum, cherry; grapes, melons, strawberries, &c. are in abundance. The whole country, indeed, seems naturally designed for the grape, the silkworm and the olive.

Barnwell is a well watered district. The Edisto washes the north-eastern side, is famous for its lumber, and is navigable for good sized boats ;—the Savannah borders it on the south-west, which admits the passage of large steam boats the whole length of the district. It is penetrated, and partially traversed in the center by the Salkehatchie, the main stream of which is now opened by art, for the passage of rafts and small boats. Besides these, there are many smaller streams by which the district is abundantly watered. Such are the smaller Salkehatchie, an arm from the greater stream; the Three Runs, Jackson's Branch, and the head branches of the Coosawhatchie. The Clear Ponds are bodies of water, like lakes, of considerable depth and circumference, at once beautiful to the eye, and of never failing resource in the dryest seasons. The Savannah and Edisto rivers are famous for their fish. In the former the shad; in the latter, the trout, rock and cat, are found in great abundance. The smaller streams also yield many fine varieties, trout, perch, bream, red-horse, &c.

The climate of Barnwell, except in the immediate neighborhood of the river swamps, is considered healthy. In these situations, bilious fevers prevail in autumn. The temperature is mild and warm; the air during the winter and spring is particularly congenial to those troubled with pulmonary affections. The town of Aiken is a famous retreat for persons suffering from these complaints, particularly in the summer. Another place of summer resort is Boiling Springs.

Barnwell district once formed a part of Orangeburg. It was known as Winton. It was first, but imperfectly, settled in 1704. In 1800, it was made an independent judicial district. Its population has advanced with far greater rapidity than most of the other districts of the state. In 1800, it had a total of 7,286 persons; in 1820, 14,750; by the census of 1840, it has 21,471. It is entitled to one senator and four representatives in the state legislature. [*See statistics of* 1840.]

This district is making large strides towards improvement. A more various and better cultivation of the soil is in progress. A greater attention is paid to the education of the young. An agricultural society has been established, which holds frequent meetings and an annual fair at the district town. In the town of Aiken, a military, scientific and classical school has just been established; and there are numerous other schools at Boiling Springs, Barnwell, Aiken and other places. The poor house fund is appropriated to the support of an establishment; but the poor are not numerous. The religious denominations are chiefly the Baptists, the Methodists, and Presbyterians. There is a Roman Catholic church at the town of Barnwell, but the community is small.

The chief towns are, Barnwell, (which is the district town,) Aiken, Blackville and Grahamville. There are several smaller settlements, such as Williston and Midway. All of these, with the exception of Barnwell, are upon the line of the Charleston and Hamburg rail road, which runs nearly fifty miles through this district. Barnwell is a pleasant village, near the center of the district, sixty miles from Columbia, and one hundred from Charleston. It contains the court-house, jail, an academy, some handsome private dwellings, and about 750 inhabitants. It is stationary.

Aiken, which is one hundred and twenty miles from Charleston, is a place of considerable and increasing importance. It is remarkable for its health, its bracing, dry atmosphere, which makes it a place of retreat for invalids. Being in the line of rail road, intersected by stage routes for the mountains, it is almost equally easy of access from Charleston, Augusta and Greenville. It possesses a number of fine dwelling-houses, several churches, several excellently kept taverns, and is particularly famous for its Coker spring, a fountain of delicious water, which is equally cold and unfailing.

Blackville is a flourishing village, with several stores, and about 150 inhabitants. It is ninety-one miles from Charleston, and ten to Barnwell court-house.

The history of Barnwell district, during the revolutionary war, is almost a blank. It was then little more than a frontier, with very few inhabitants, unexplored, and without public roads. The most important settlement was Fort Dreadnought, afterwards Fort Galphin, at Silver Bluff. This fort was established by the old colonial government as a check upon the Indians. The tribe of Euchees occupied the neighborhood. Galphin, a famous Indian trader, lived here for many years. Silver Bluff is one of the curiosities of the district. It rises many feet perpendicularly above the Savannah river, which winds along its base. This steep bank, rising thus abruptly, discovers many curious strata of earth, mixed with different clays and shells;—and earths apparently of an aluminous or vitriolic nature. Here also are found pyrites, sulphurous and other fragments, shining like brass; as also petrified sticks, limbs and trunks of trees; leaves, acorns and their cups,—all of which are as hard and shining as charcoal.

BEAUFORT DISTRICT.

Beaufort District forms the south-western corner of the state. It is bounded on the north-east by Colleton; on the north-west by Barnwell; on the south-west by the Savannah river; and on the south and south-east by the Atlantic ocean. The length of the district, from south to north, is fifty-eight miles; breadth from east to west, thirty-three miles; it contains 1,224,960 acres. It comprises four parishes; viz:—St. Helena, St. Luke, St. Peter and Prince William.

The soil is equally various and valuable. Nearly one half of the territory is rich swamp land, susceptible of easy improvement, and capable of great production. Rich, deep, broad tracts of loam, border the numerous streams and rivers, in some places of inexhaustible fertility; but its population is not sufficiently dense for its adequate improvement and reclamation. The high lands between the swamps are of a light but productive nature; chiefly of sand, bottomed upon clay, which lies about two feet deep. The numerous islands which stud the Atlantic margin of this district, are also of a light, sandy, but fertile description. These islands are numerous; some of them famous for their production of long staple cotton, to which they give their name of sea-island; others are almost equally famous among the residents, as hunting grounds. Many of them are beautiful to the eye and salubrious as well as rich. A few of the most remarkable may be named. Upon the sea-coast are Reynolds', Prentis, Chaplin, Edings, Hilton, Dawfuskie and Turtle. Between these and the main, are St. Helena, Pinckney, Parris, Port Royal, Ladies, Bermuda, Morgan, Calwassee, Lemon, Coosaw, and many others. The rivers are equally numerous. The shores are indented by numerous arms of the sea, and navigable water courses are frequent. The principal are, the Savannah, Broad, Combahee, Coosaw, Port Royal, May, Colleton, Morgan, Bull, Cooper, Chee-chee-see and Tulifinnee. The Broad is an arm of the sea, an extraordinary body of water, forming a bay, or sound, in some places more than two miles wide.

The face of Beaufort district is uniformly level. The climate, though moist and hot, is healthy compared with the other districts on the sea-board of South Carolina. Its sea-islands are supposed to be quite healthy, and the sand ridges between the swamps and water courses are equally so. The town of Beaufort has always been remarkable for the health and longevity of the inhabitants.

Beaufort lies within the alluvial country, and is without rock of any kind. There is a hard substance occasionally found, resembling marble, which is evidently formed of shells. A rock of this substance lies at the junction of the rivers New and Cooper. Shells and the remains of marine animals are found in abundance.

The waters, salt and fresh, abound in the finest fish. In the former are caught, drum, bass, black, sheep's-head, whiting, cavalli, mullet, sailor's-choice, &c.—of shell-fish, sea-turtle, oysters, crabs, shrimps, &c. The fresh waters produce, pike, perch, and other varieties.

The timber trees are, live and other oaks, pine, cypress, red-cedar, hickory, magnolia, palmetto, poplar, beech, birch, ash, &c. Of the fruit trees there are, the orange, sweet and sour; peach, nectarine, fig, and cherry. The grapes and fruit berries are numerous.

The game, beasts and birds, includes,—of the former, the deer, wild cat, fox, otter, squirrel, rabbit, opossum, raccoon, &c.—of the latter, the eagle, hawk, crow, owl, parroquet, rice-bird, duck, turkey, pigeon, curlew, flamingo, woodcock, goose, dove, &c.

The singing birds are, the mocker, nonpareil, blue-bird, linnet and red-bird.

The serpents are, the rattle-snake, viper, black, moccasin, copper, water, &c. The alligator, in great size and number, inhabits the fresh and brackish waters.

The productions of Beaufort are, cotton, (long and short,) rice, Indian corn, wheat, oats, rye, barley and potatoes. Sugar and indigo have been raised at particular periods. Castor oil is still produced in small quantities. There is a good winter and summer pasturage for cattle. The domestic manufactures are few; and the commerce of the district is confined to a few sloops and schooners in the coastwise trade.

Beaufort district is remarkable in the history of the state, as being the seat of the earliest settlements ever made in the country. The French or Huguenot colonies, under Ribault and Landonniere, were made in this district in 1562. They made settlements on St. Helena, and other places, but were destroyed by the Spaniards under Melendez. Their history is a singularly interesting one. Remains of their settlements, old forts, and even cannon, have been found. Some portions of the forts may be seen to this day.

The English, in 1670, under Sayle, made settlements at St. Helena, which they abandoned for Ashley river.

In 1682, lord Cardross attempted a settlement at Port Royal island, with a small colony from Scotland, which was dislodged by an invasion of Spaniards from St. Augustine. The first permanent settlement was made in 1700. Beaufort no doubt owes its name to a French origin.

The population of the district is 35,800. It sends one senator from each of its four parishes, and eight representatives to the state legislature.

The literary and educational institutions of Beaufort are good. The intellectual reputation of the people is very high. In the town of Beaufort there is a valuable library, and a highly refined and well educated society. The Baptists are the most numerous religious sect. There are also respectable communities of Episcopalians, Methodists and Presbyterians.

Beaufort is the principal town in the district. It lies at the head of Port Royal river, is regularly laid out and has been handsomely improved. The private dwellings are numerous and neat. Its harbor, about fifteen miles from the sea, is one of the greatest depth and space in the southern country; but the ease with which it may be entered, and the difficulty of fortifying it against an enemy, have prevented its being made use of as a governmental depot; with a populous and productive interior country, Beaufort would seem to be particularly eligible as a great commercial seat. The population is about 1,600.

Gillisonville is now the district town of the district; formerly it was Coosawhatchie. The unhealthiness of the latter place, led to the occupation of the former as the seat of public justice. Gillisonville has a fine court-house, jail, tavern, and several private dwellings. Coosawhatchie lies at the head of sloop navigation on the river, from which it takes its name. The name is Indian, and marked the site of a populous Indian village. A thriving business has been done in this place, the population of which is about 250. It is seventy-two miles from Charleston, and one hundred and twenty from Columbia.

The Purrysburg settlement was made by a Swiss colony, in 1732. It is well situated, on a high bluff on the Savannah river, twenty miles north of the city of Savannah. It is a small and not a prosperous village.

Robertville is a village pleasantly situated on a rising ground, about five miles from the Savannah river, and twenty-three miles below the Barnwell line. It is a thriving village, with a church, post-office, academy, a public library, and carries on a brisk trade with the neighboring country.

Pocotaligo is an old village, established as a place of trade long before the revolution. It stands upon the river of its own name, in the parish of Prince William. It has now dwindled into an unimportant hamlet. In 1712 it contained 300 inhabitants. It was here that the Yémassee Indians first commenced their bloody operations in the famous Indian outbreak of 1715, which threatened the destruction of the whole province. The British fort, Balfour, at this place, was gallantly captured by an inferior American force, under colonel Harden. There are several other small hamlets, employed as summer retreats, in the district;—Grahamville, Rockspring, McPherson, and Heywardsville; but in winter they are unoccupied.

Beaufort has been the mother of several very eminent men; among these, William Bull, who was several times entrusted with the administration of the provincial government. Colonel John Barnwell was a successful partisan leader, and distinguished himself against the Indians in several wars. Another Barnwell of the same name, acquired reputation in the revolution. Colonel Robert Barnwell is also favorably known in this war. Colonel Harden, also of this district, was particularly conspicuous as a cavalry officer, of great acuteness, bravery and activity. He was an associate of Sumter and Marion, and worthy of such generals.

CHARLESTON DISTRICT.

CHARLESTON DISTRICT is bounded on the north by the districts of Sumter and Williamsburg; on the north-east by Williamsburg and Georgetown; on the south and east by the Atlantic ocean; on the north-west by Orangeburg; and on the west and south-west by Colleton. It is the largest district in the state; contains the metropolis; presents a line of coast on the ocean of seventy-four miles; extends fifty-three miles into the interior, and embraces an area of 1,351,680 acres. In these extensive limits are included a large number of valuable islands. The most important among these are, Sullivan, James', Daniel, Morrison, Bull, Owendaw, Seewee, Edisto, John, Wadmalaw, Folly, Seabrook, Keawah, Johassee and Copahee. The sea-coast of this district is indented with numerous creeks and inlets. The principal rivers are, the Santee, Edisto, Ashley, (Keawah,) Cooper, (Etiwan,) Wando, Stono, Dawhoo, Wadmalaw, &c. The confluence of the Cooper and Ashley, forms the bay and harbor of Charleston city. The Cooper, which lies wholly in this district, is navigable nearly to its sources. The Ashley is navigable for small vessels as far as Bacon's bridge. The Santee river, which is one of the most important in the state, forms the north and north-eastern boundary of the district. It is remarkable for the rich soil upon its borders; its productive rice plantations, and the frequent freshets by which its low lands are devastated for awhile and finally enriched. With its tributaries, the Saluda, the Congaree and Wateree, it is navigable for more than six hundred miles. The Santee has a good steamboat navigation to its junction with the two latter rivers. It enters the ocean by two mouths. It is famous for its fish.

The inlets are, those of Charleston, South Santee, Stono, north and south Edisto, Price, Capers and Dewees.

The bays are, Bull and Sewee.

Cape Roman, a well known mark for seamen, is in this district. Copakee sound, the only one in the district, lies in Christ church parish.

The soil of Charleston district is of very various character, from the richest vegetable and marine mould, to the most barren and unproductive sands. The swamps, when embanked or reclaimed, are of inexhaustible fertility. Along the rivers, this character of richness continues to mark the soil; but the upland ridges between are poor, consisting chiefly of sands, pine land tracts, now and then sprinkled with swamps, green savannahs, and small knolls and ridges of vegetable loam, which are very productive. This district lies wholly within the alluvial region. The lower part is entirely free from rocks or even pebbles, except the shell limestone, which is to be seen in many places, particularly in the neighborhood of Eutaw springs, where it may be found in blocks of considerable size. They appear, also, near Harley's bridge, on the waters of Four Hole swamp. No minerals have been discovered in this district. Occasionally there have been some appearances of iron. A quarry of iron sandstone, near Pineville, was employed in the construction of the locks for the Santee canal.

The waste lands of this district are very valuable and very extensive. They might with ease be made to support an additional population of one hundred thousand persons. Unhappily, the climate, in the richest portions, is unfavorable to European life. These waste lands consist of unreclaimed swamp and marsh, deserted rice fields, inland bays, and a large extent of pine barren. Proper draining, by a population sufficiently numerous, would no doubt greatly improve the health of this now neglected region.

The chief productions are, rice and the several varieties of cotton. The soil and climate of Charleston district are well adapted, in addition to these, to the growth of indigo, flax, madder, maize, rye, barley, &c. ; potato, turnip, tanya, carrot, onion, &c. The garden-farms in the neighborhood of the metropolis, are only partially maintained in cultivation, and do not supply its wants. Large sums are annually and unwisely sent abroad for grain, vegetables and forage, which, with proper care and diligence, might be raised in ample quantities at home. Among the articles thus imported, are, corn, hay, cabbages, onions, &c. The *pasturage* of Charleston is good; but the yield of beef, mutton, veal, pork, poultry, butter, and other commodities of a like nature, though considerable, is totally inadequate to the consumption of the city.

The forest and fruit trees of this district comprise nearly all the varieties which are to be found in any other. Among these are, the several kinds of oak, the pine, the cypress, the magnolia, the hickory, the gum, the palmetto, &c. The fruit trees are, the peach, the pear, the plum, the apple, the orange, the nectarine, the fig, &c,—besides the grape, the melon, the may-apple, and the usual varieties of fruit-berry.

The fish of this district are abundant and of many kinds. The trout, bream, perch, cat, rock, pike, carp or suck, herring, silver, gar and eel, inhabit the fresh waters ;—the salt water fish, which are equally plentiful, are equally various. Among them are, the shark, porpoise, drum, bass, whiting, sailor's choice, cavalli, shad, black, porgy, mullet, skipjack, crocus, sheep's-head, &c. The shell fish, salt and fresh, are, the turtle, terrapin, crab, oyster, clam, shrimp, &c. The birds and reptiles may be found under the head of the natural history of the state, and are those, generally, which are found in every part of it.

The climate of Charleston district is mild and agreeable in winter; in summer, hot, moist and unhealthy. Along the sea-coast, the temperature during the warmer months of the year, is rendered more agreeable by the prevalence of the ocean breezes, which also contribute to render certain situations upon the sea-board salubrious, and highly desirable as places of resort during the sickly season. Such is Sullivan's island. The atmosphere is generally relieved, when the weather is intensely warm, by the almost daily occurrence of grateful showers, accompanied by much thunder and lightning. Along the pine ridges, between the water courses, frequent situations are found where the most perfect health may be enjoyed at all seasons. These are places of resort, and form the summer villages of the planters, during the months of June, July, August, September and October; at all other periods they are abandoned.

The district of Charleston is sub-divided into ten parishes, viz.—St. Stephen, St. James, (Goose Creek,) St. James, (Santee,) St. John, (Berkley,) St. Thomas, Christ Church, St. John, (Colleton,) St. Andrew, St. Philip and St. Michael. The two last comprise the city and suburbs of Charleston. These parishes are constituted seperate election and municipal districts. Their population, according to the census of 1840, is as follows: St. Philip and St. Michael, (comprising the city of Charleston and the Neck,) 41,149; St. James, (Goose Creek,) 4,131; St. John, (Berkley,) 10,513; St. Stephen, 2,483; St. James, (Santee,) 2,932; Christ Church, 2,589; St. Thomas, 2,890; St. Andrew, 4,434; St. John, (Colleton,) 11,582; making a grand total of 82,673.

Cities and Villages. Charleston is the chief city of the district and of the state; the suburb, called the Neck, which immediately adjoins the city, is the next community in importance, but remains unincorporated, and is in all respects, taxation and internal police alone excepted, a portion of the city.

Moultrieville, in Christ Church parish, is at the entrance of Charleston harbor, on Sullivan's island. It contains a large summer population, being the place of retreat for the citizens of Charleston during the sickly season. At such times it has one thousand persons, increasing in proportion to the degree of sickness which may prevail in the city. It has its churches, market, town-hall, mayor and wardens; and a steamboat, and sometimes two, plies at intervals throughout the day, during the summer, between it and the city. Its exposed situation, however—open to the sea—which secures its salubrity, subjects it to the unimpeded action of the elements; and the storms of September have done fearful mischief upon its shores, and sometimes upon its inhabitants; the island itself, was, in 1822, in danger of being submerged; several lives were lost; but a change of wind and the subsiding of the sea, providentially defeated the danger.

Mount Pleasant, on the east side of Charleston harbor; Fort Johnson in St. Andrews parish, and Edingsville on Edings island, are agreeable retreats during summer. The latter contains two churches and two or three hundred inhabitants. Pineville, in St. Stephen's parish, has a considerable population, and has long been famous as a place of healthy summer residence—a character somewhat impaired in later days. This region was originally settled by the French Huguenots, a gentle and noble people, whose descendants still maintain the virtues which rendered their ancestors so much beloved. The remaining villages are few and small; mostly temporary; used only as contiguous plantation retreats during the summer.

The Indian names of this district, which are still preserved, are numerous, and indicate the various tribes by which the country was occupied; such are the Santee, the Wando, the Etiwan, (Cooper,) the Keawah, (Ashley,) Wappoo, Wassamasaw, Eutaw, Wappetaw, Wappoolaw, Wahkenaw, and many others.

Charleston district has been well marked by the footsteps of war. Scarce a mile of her territory that has not been watered by the blood of her sons. Charleston itself has been several times beleaguered. The Indian tribes of the south, the Yemassee, the Stono, the Savannah, and others, have carried their arms to her gates; the Spaniards made a similar approach, bringing the Indians with them as allies. Twice was she besieged by the British, once by Provost, and the second time, when she was captured, by Clinton and Arbuthnot. Many were the places throughout the district noted for sharp and bloody battles. That of Fort Moultrie is famous; the battle of Eutaw is scarcely less so; then follow the fierce conflicts of Stono, Monk's Corner, Quinby, Biggin, Nelson's, Rantole's, Strawberry ferry, and the Quarter house, for all of which see the History of South Carolina. Many were her famous names, before, during, and since the revolution. She has good reason to be proud of her sons; conspicuous among whom are the family names of Moultrie, Rutledge, Marion, Lowndes, Drayton, Pinckney, Huger, Horry, Grimke, Middleton, &c. She has maintained high rank in politics, in letters, in arts and sciences. In every department of excellence, indeed, she has urged high and indisputable claims to rank with the most noble sections of the whole nation.

The militia of Charleston district consists of one brigade, comprising four regiments and one battalion of artillery. It is entitled to two senators and seventeen representatives in the state legislature, and one member in the Congress of the United States.

The natural curiosities of Charleston district are few and unimportant. The Eutaw springs are much more celebrated as the scene of a fierce revolutionary battle, than for their waters. The spring rises through a small opening in the earth, only a few inches in diameter, and immediately forms a basin of transparent water, a few feet deep, but about one hundred and fifty paces round. Thence, penetrating a subterraneous passage, it percolates through a ridge of porous limestone or concretion of large oyster shells, and at a distance of an hundred paces or more, boils up, and bubbling through a variety of passages, forms the head of Eutaw creek, which, running north-westwardly for about two miles, finds its way into Santee river. Bones of singular dimensions, belonging to some unknown animal, have been found in the neighborhood of the Santee, in this district, while digging some nine feet below the surface. Some idea of the monster to which the bones belonged, may be formed by the following: One rib was nearly six feet long, a tooth eight inches in length, three and a half in width, with a root of eleven and a half inches more. The rest that may be said of this district, will be best placed under the head of the

CITY OF CHARLESTON.

The history of Charleston, if properly written, would make a most interesting volume by itself. It has been, in many respects, the mother of the south. Its sons, arms and money, have been freely supplied, at almost every call, to the sister states and cities. Its troops have fought at the gates of St. Augustine, at the waters of Mobile, by the Roanoke and the Ohio. Conspicuously situated for action, it was at once the distinguished mark for enemies, the rallying point and place of refuge for friends and allies. It was invaded, when in its most infant state, by the French and Spaniards, by whom the neighboring Indians were continually stimulated to the wild and bloody work of murder and insurrection. For a long period, the Ashley river settlement was the object of peculiar heart-burning to the hostile powers of Europe, and of hope and fear, and exultation, to the proprietary and crown authorities.

The city of Charleston is the seat of justice of the district, and the commercial emporium of the state. It is well placed for commerce, at the confluence of Ashley and Cooper rivers, just where, forming a common mouth, they are about to empty themselves into the sea. The ocean rolls in sight, as it were before her doors, but six miles distant, but shut out from violent intrusion by long arms of sand, islands that stretching out on either hand, forms a capacious basin, in which the city sits equally conspicuous and secure. The rivers which form this beautiful bay, run a parallel course for nearly six miles; broadening at every step, and thus gradually narrowing the city into a complete peninsula. There are few finer objects of sight, of this description, than the bay of Charleston. The width of the inner harbor, at its mouth, is little over a mile. On either hand, this passage is guarded by three fortresses, judiciously placed, to delay and destroy an enemy. On one side is Fort Moultrie, on Sullivan's island; on the other side is Fort Johnson, on James' island. In front of the city, and partially between it and the entrance, is castle Pinckney. To these a fourth is to be added, which is now in progress, formed upon a mole, in the sea, and close upon the channel; a structure likely to be more efficient than either of the former, in arresting the passage of an enemy. This is to be called Fort Sumter, and though as yet incomplete, can readily, in the event of any emergency, be made to receive another palmetto battery like that which, on the 28th June, 1776, silenced and gave America her FIRST victory over a British fleet, and drove them out to sea in disastrous defeat. The outer harbor lying within the bar, extends about six miles,—from Sullivan's island to the south channel, below the light house. The bar, which is one partial source of the security of Charleston from invasion, is yet a serious obstruction in the way of its commerce. It is formed by an accumulation of sand banks, which have been deposited from time to time by storms, and which are only kept from becoming a permanent island by the operation of the tides, the rush of the downward rivers, and the land wash in heavy rains. There are three channels for entrance to the harbor—the ship channel, which has sixteen feet of water at ebb tide; the over-all, or middle channel, which has twelve to fourteen feet water; and Lawford's, or the south channel, which has but nine feet. Two other channels are found, but not used unless by coasters, having not more than from four to eight feet water. The ship channel is eleven miles and a half from the city; the middle or direct channel, but seven and a half. The approach to the coast is easy, the soundings gradual, and on entering the middle channel, you look, free of any interruption, directly into the inner harbor, and command a complete view of the city, guided by the tall

CITY OF CHARLESTON. 51

spire of St. Michael's church, which bears from this point about N. 63 W. The light-house, which fronts the ship channel, is a lofty brick tower, containing a revolving light.

The latitude of Charleston is 32° 45' N. long. 1° 8' 30" E. of Columbia 2° 57' 3" W. of the Capitol at Washington, and 79° 52' 3" W. of Greenwich Observatory.

The population of the city of Charleston proper, by the census of 1840, is as follows:—White males, 6,826; white females, 6,203 : total whites, 13,029. Free colored males, 584 ; free colored females, 977 : total free colored, 1,561. Male slaves, 6,334; female slaves, 8,339 : total slaves, 14,673. Aggregate total, 29,263.

Charleston Neck.—White males, 1,766 ; white females, 1,685 : total white persons, 3,441. Free colored males, 525 ; free colored females, 683 : total free colored persons, 1,208. Male slaves, 3,376 ; female slaves, 3,781 : total slaves, 7,127. Aggregrate total, 11,876. Grand total of Charleston city and Neck, 41,149.

The occupations of the people of Charleston are chiefly those of trade and mechanics. A large portion of her residents, however, are those who carry on agricultural interests in the neighboring parishes. Its first settlement was in 1671. In its original condition, it was low, intersected with numerous creeks and marshes, which time and industry have almost entirely reclaimed. The growth of the city was tardy from the beginning, discouraged by war, pestilence and other disasters. In 1704, the boundaries of the city did not extend farther west than Meeting street;—north, than the present Market street, and south, than Water street. All this region was environed by a line of fortifications. Now, the whole area, from river to river, is reclaimed and covered with dwellings, and from the extreme south point of the peninsula, it extends nearly two miles north. Its whole eastern extent is now faced with wharves, which are in turn lined with solid and spacious fabrics, all of brick, devoted wholly to the purposes of trade, and corresponding with the commerce of the city, and with the vast bulk and great value of the staple of the country, of which the city is the agent. All this extent of wharfing may be seen, during the winter and spring, made populous with shipping, displaying the flags of all portions of the world. The difficulties of the bar once overcome, the harbor of Charleston furnishes a safe and spacious anchorage, with a depth of water capable of almost any burden. The business portions of the city are paved with stone, the side walks of brick, and occasionally other streets; but there are still many that remain, and need, to share in this wholesome improvement. The whole city is penetrated by drains, under ground, by which the waters are carried off, and the refuse of the streets discharged into the contiguous rivers.

The city of Charleston was incorporated in 1783. It is divided into four wards, all of which are represented in a board consisting of a mayor and twelve aldermen. Its municipal regulations are very strict and well conceived. Its quiet at night is rather that of a country village than of a commercial city. This effect is produced as much by the high social life among its inhabitants as by its police. The city has a military guard or night-watch, consisting of more than one hundred men, (some of whom are mounted,) with the proper complement of officers. A volunteer guard appears in arms, in the event of fire. Charleston has suffered very much from fire. Its present excellent regulations, which forbid the erection of wooden houses, is calculated to increase her securities. An additional source of security is in her fire companies, which are numerous, very respectable and vigilant, emulous in a high degree of each other, and consist of stout courageous young men, whose equal pride and patriotism, stimulate to the most daring performances in moments of danger.

The public buildings of Charleston, are numerous and frequently imposing. The public taste in architecture has undergone great improvement in late years. Something however is still lacking in this respect. St. Michael's church steeple, an old British work, still claims pre-eminence for its exquisite proportions, as well as for its great height above all the other public buildings of Charleston. St. Philip's, destroyed within a few years, has been rebuilt, partially after the old plan, that of the form of a cross, but modified with some new improvements. The Theatre, Market-House, Jewish Synagogue, Hibernian Hall, Charleston hotel, all new structures, are all highly creditable to the city and the architects by whom they were designed. Numerous other buildings, public and private, within a few years, denote great improvement in public taste, and a great increase of public enterprise. The churches of Charleston are numerous; and many of them very spacious and well planned. Among these, including St. Michael's and St. Philip's, already mentioned, are six devoted to the Episcopal persuasion, three Presbyterian; four Methodist; one Jewish; three Roman Catholic; two German; two Baptist; one Unitarian; one French Calvinist; one Universalist; one Mariner's; one Congregationalist; and one Orphan—in all, twenty-six. The buildings devoted to public business, are the Court House and Exchange, fine old fashioned samples of solid workmanship and good proportion; the State Offices, (fire proof,) the City Hall, State Citadel, Orphan House, Guard House, Charleston Library, Charleston College, Theatre, Hibernian Hall, St. Andrew's Hall, Medical College, Apprentices' Library, Marine Hospital, Market Hall and Gaol.

The banks are seven in number, viz.—The Charleston Bank, the Bank of the State, (a state institution,) the Planter's and Mechanic's Bank, the State Bank, the Bank of South Carolina, the Union Bank and the Rail Road Bank. The united capital of these institutions is about ten millions of dollars. The rail road, beginning on the confines of the city and extending by two branches, one to Hamburg, one hundred and thirty-six miles, the other to Columbia one hundred and thirty miles, is a work of great local utility and general convenience. In an isolated part of the suburbs, about two miles from the city, the state has erected nine fire-proof magazines for keeping the public powder, and as depositories for that of merchants. These buildings are circular in form, with conical roofs, and disposed in three ranges. They are of brick, rough-cast. The center building, meant exclusively for the public powder, is the largest, and will contain four thousand kegs. The roof is bomb-proof. The other buildings can, each, contain one thousand kegs.

The charitable institutions are numerous and active. Among them, the Orphan House, an old and noble charity, is conspicuous. It has seldom less than two hundred and fifty inmates of both sexes, who are carefully fed, clothed and educated. A board of commissioners, a steward, matron and physician, regularly superintend or periodically examine the institution. The South Carolina and Fellowship societies are charities of like character, confined, however, to the children and families of members. The Hibernian and St. Patrick's society, address themselves to the care of providing for the wants of emigrant Irish; the St. Andrew's society devote themselves in like manner, to the needy Scotch; the St. George, to the English sufferer, and the German Friendly society, with great effect and activity, to the poor German emigrant. Besides these, there are numerous other institutions and societies, more or less able, who all equally devote themselves to benevolent works. The Poor-House, (which is a city institution;) the Society for the relief of Widows and Orphans of the Clergy of the Protestant Episcopal Church; the Marine Hospital, (a national institution;) Shirra's Dispensary, and many more, reflect honor on the country and community, and increase its claims to regard, as a noble working Christian people.

The people of Charleston have always shown themselves properly mindful of the subject of education. They have spared neither pains nor money to secure for their children its wondrous benefits. The private schools are numerous for both sexes, mostly efficient and improving. There are five public or free schools, for the children of the indigent, for which the state appropriates annually about five thousand dollars. The city has established a College, which is well organized and has already, though but a few years in operation, brought forth good fruits. The faculty consists of a president and two professors, assisted by one tutor. The High School, more recently founded by the city, is a highly valuable and useful institution, independent of the College; but an excellent natural auxiliary in preparing young gentlemen for its walls. Both are likely to be as successful as they certainly are useful and important. The Charleston Medical College is flourishing at the head of all the medical schools in the whole south. It ranks below none in the Union. The number of students is now never less than one hundred and fifty. The Apprentices' Library Society, is one of the most valuable educational institutions of the city, particularly addressed to the young mechanic, furnishing him with books free of charge, in every department of letters; and occasionally informing him, by means of lecture and illustration, in arts and sciences, which he could not so readily comprehend in books. The library of this society contains ten thousand volumes, all the gift of private individuals. The Charleston Library contains eighteen thousand volumes. This library, when it had seven thousand volumes, had the misfortune to be destroyed by fire. In this fire it lost, beside its books, a valuable collection of paintings. Its loss in certain departments of literature, has never been entirely repaired. It possesses now several valuable pictures, and an extensive cabinet of curiosities. To the Charleston and the Medical Colleges, and High School, are also attached considerable libraries, and some few of private gentlemen are said to reach eight thousand volumes. The city circulating libraries, are also numerous. The literary clubs of Charleston are numerous. The periodicals, are a quarterly Review, two monthly and several weekly periodicals. The newspapers are six in number, and for good writing, just thinking and propriety of manner, are among the first in the whole Union. The first Charleston newspaper was printed in 1738.

The trade and commerce of Charleston are of great importance. The following table will show her domestic exports for twenty years.

DOMESTIC EXPORTS OF SOUTH CAROLINA FROM 1819 TO 1841.

Years	Exports.	Years.	Exports.	Years.	Exports.
1820	8,690,539	1827	8,189,496	1834	11,119,565
1821	6,867,515	1828	6,508,570	1835	11,224,298
1822	7,136,366	1829	8,134,676	1836	13,482,757
1823	6,671,998	1830	7,580,821	1837	11,138,992
1824	7,833,713	1831	6,528,605	1838	11,017,391
1825	10,876,475	1832	7,685,833	1839	10,318,822
1826	7,468,966	1833	8,337,512	1840	10,036,769
	55,545,572		52,965,513		78,338,594

Gain in last seven years, 25,373,081.

Her own shipping bears no proportion to her productions, and has been much greater at an earlier period than now. Ship building was commenced in Charleston prior to 1740. Before the revolution, she had built more than twenty-five square rigged vessels, and many more of smaller burden. Her carrying trade has been taken out of her hands. British and northern bottoms absorb it all. Occasionally, the public spirit of an individual citizen has attempted to repair this deficiency, but without much success. The enterprise of the people inclines them rather to agriculture and to trade; and this is not to be complained of at a period when the passion for trade has drawn so many, there and in other parts of the country, from the slower but safer business of agriculture. The energies of Charleston have been chiefly directed to the extension of her commerce into the interior. To some extent this has been done by means of the Hamburg and Columbia rail roads. Numerous steamboats ply from this city to Savannah, Beaufort, Georgetown,

Columbia, St. Augustine and other places ; and, no doubt, with the return of public prosperity, the work of domestic enterprise will be resumed, so as to increase the facilities for intercourse with the numerous towns of the interior, of Georgia, Alabama and Florida, upon which so much of the commercial prosperity of Charleston depends.

CHESTER DISTRICT.

The District of CHESTER lies within the granite region of the state. It is bounded on the west by Broad river, which separates it from Union district; east by Lancaster; north by York; and south by Fairfield. The average length of Chester is thirty-one, and its breadth eighteen and one-fourth miles. It contains 361,600 acres. The soil of this district is various and fertile; containing a large proportion of clay, with a covering of vegetable matter, more or less mixed with primitive substances. The ridges between the water courses are sandy, with other light soil. The low grounds are sometimes stony, with little gravel and much rich loam. The face of the country is hilly, abounding with the finest granite and soap stone. No minerals or metals have been discovered. The rivers are, the Broad and the Catawba, both of which are navigable for boats the whole length of the district; the smaller streams, which are not navigable in consequence of the rapidity of their currents are, the Rocky, Fishing, Turkey and Sandy rivers, the two first of which are branches of the Catawba, the two last of Broad river, and all of which have numerous and beautiful branches in turn. The falls of the Catawba are a great natural curiosity. These are situated above Rocky Mount. The descending stream is confined by rocks which rise in height, and approach each other gradually, like walls, narrowing the river from a stream an hundred and eighty yards wide, into a channel of less than sixty. Through this channel it is forced down into the narrowest part of the stream, called the 'Gulf,' where, pent up on every side but one, it rushes over rocky steeps and ledges, is dashed from rock to rock, and forming a sheet of foam from shore to shore, is precipitated over no less than twenty falls, to a depth of nearly one hundred and fifty feet. The agitated waters finally subside into partial tranquility, in a stream of more than three hundred yards in width. The scenery here is very grand and beautiful.

The fish in the waters of Chester are, the shad, trout, red-horse, cat, perch, eel, rock-fish, and many others.

The forests contain few pines, and these are of the short leaf; the most common native trees are, the several varieties of oak, the walnut, beech, poplar, &c. The fruits are, the apple, peach, pear and plum, all of which thrive with little or no cultivation. Cotton is the chief commodity of culture, but there is no neglect of the grain and provision crops. The game are, the deer, fox and turkey, the rabbit, squirrel, raccoon and opossum, all of which are in great numbers. The shad desert the rivers in the fall and return with the spring.

Chester was first settled in 1750, chiefly by emigrants from Pennsylvania and Virginia. It takes its name from a county in the former state. A considerable accession of Irish settlers was made to its population in 1763, after the peace of Paris. Indeed, the greater portion of the inhabitants of the district may trace their descent from the Irish. The population by the last census, (1840,) is 17,747; of these, 10,025 are free, and 7,722 slaves; showing an increase, in twenty years, of nearly 4,000 inhabitants. Chester is entitled to one senator and four representatives in the state legislature.

The district town is Chesterville. It is beautifully placed upon the dividing ridge between the waters of the Broad and Catawba rivers, at the head of the east branch of Sandy river. The situation is lofty and romantic, and so commanding, that it has been likened to one of the strong fortresses of the feudal times and barons—a little San Marino, equally secure in position, as in the possession of a free, fearless and contented population. The grounds about it slope on all sides in the manner of a glacis; the woods are cleared beyond the range of cannon shot. The town contains a handsome Court-House, an Academy, a Jail, and about 250 inhabitants. Education is improving. The state annually appropriates twelve hundred dollars for the instruction of the poor. The number of the dependent poor is very small,—not more than twenty-five; they are supported by the charity of the district. In 1825, the blind were fifteen; deaf and dumb, seven; and lunatic, three. The climate of Chester, though variable, is esteemed healthy and invigorating. Of the religious sects, the Presbyterian is the most numerous; after this, the Methodist and Baptist. Mount Dearborn was the name given to a military establishment of the United States, at Rocky Mount, which was afterwards abandoned. It is a beautiful and imposing position. The manufactures of this district are wholly domestic. Colonel Lacy, who distinguished himself at the battles of Hanging Rock, King's Mountain and Blackstock's, was a native of Chester. It was in this district, near the waters of the Eswawpuddenah, that Sumter defeated the British under Weyms; and here, also, on the banks of Fishing Creek, this brave patriot met a severe reverse; suffering a surprise, by which his troops were totally routed. For these actions, see the History of South Carolina.

CHESTERFIELD DISTRICT.

This District, like that of Chester, was settled by emigrants from Pennsylvania and Virginia. It is matter of regret that the names of the two should seem to have been drawn from the same sources. It is stated, however, that Chesterfield derives its name from that of the accomplished Earl,—an assertion, the proofs of which are beyond our reach. Chesterfield constitutes one part of the northern boundary of the state. In this quarter, it is bounded by the state of North Carolina; on the east by Marlborough; on the south-east by Darlington, and on the south-west by Kershaw and Lancaster districts. It averages, in length, thirty-one miles; in breadth, twenty-six; and contains about 515,840 square acres. The face of the country is various and undulating. The upper part of it lies within the granite region, and contains an abundance of this kind of rock. Here is also to be found asbestos, which is incombustible; slate and freestone; but no limestone, or other calcareous matter.

The nature of the soil, in a large proportion of this district, is sandy and unproductive. In the neighborhood of water courses, good land is occasionally to be found. Along the northern limits, the lands are of the clayey and stony kind, and present a rolling surface. The river lands are rich. The productions are corn and cotton, potatoes, wheat, rye and oats.

The navigable stream of this district is the Pedee, which is accessible to large steamboats to Cheraw, one hundred and twenty miles from the ocean. The other rivers, which are not navigable, but might be made so, are the Kaddipah, (Lynch's,) Black, Cedar, Thompson's, Juniper, Rocky, &c. The fish are, the shad, which, when in season, are caught in the Pedee;—the trout, bream, cat, eel, perch, red-horse, suck and others.

Of the forest trees, the pitch-pine is most common through three-fourths of the southern part of Chesterfield. In the northern parts, oak, hickory, ash, poplar, &c. are the most prevalent. The fruits are the peach and apple, which are in great variety and of good quality. The game are, the deer, fox, rabbit, squirrel, raccoon, opossum, &c. The birds are, the wild turkey, pigeon, duck, goose and others, common to the whole country.

The population of Chesterfield does not increase rapidly. By the census of 1820, it was 6,645. By that of 1840, it is 8,574; of these, 5,703 are free, and 2,871 slaves. The district is entitled to one senator and two representatives in the state legislature. The chief employment of the people is agriculture. Their manufactures are considerable, but wholly for domestic use. The educational institutions are increasing and improving. The number of the poor is small, and their support does not exceed in cost five hundred dollars per annum. Nearly twice that amount is allowed by the state for the free schools. The religious sects are Methodist, Presbyterian and Baptist. The Episcopalians are few.

The seat of justice bears the name of the district. It lies on the south side of Thompson's creek, a branch of the Pedee; is distant seventy-seven miles from Columbia, and one hundred and sixty-three from Charleston. It numbers nearly 400 inhabitants. A Court-House and Jail, of brick—a tasteful mode of building, and fine groves of forest trees, judiciously left within the limits of the village—give it a pleasing and inviting aspect.

Cheraw is a place of trade and the chief town of the district. It lies on the west side of the Pedee, on a plain one hundred feet above the river. Its trade with the back country of North Carolina is considerable. Its population is about 400. It has several churches, a bank, two printing offices, a covered bridge across the Pedee, and several flourishing schools. Several steamers ply between it and the cities of Charleston and

Georgetown; and the river floats are also numerous. At this time, however, the fortunes of Cheraw seem stationary.

The greatest portion of Chesterfield is healthy. The sand hill region, which is extensive, particularly so. The climate is pleasant, and except on the river low grounds, free from bilious fevers. In 1825, there was but one blind person and one lunatic in the district; no deaf or dumb.

Cheraw is the Indian name of the aborigines by which the district was occupied. It would be well substituted for that of Chesterfield. It was once famous for its bacon, of which it shipped large quantities. The Pedee is the only other Indian name which has been preserved in the district.

COLLETON DISTRICT.

COLLETON was one of the first settled places in our state. Its geographical limits at one time, including Port Royal and all the neighboring region, were distinguished by the settlements and wars of the French and Spaniards. At this time its boundaries are, on the east and north-east, Charleston; on the north-west, Orangeburg and Barnwell; on the south-west, Beaufort; and south, the Atlantic ocean. The average length of Colleton is forty-five miles; the breadth thirty-nine. It is computed to contain 1,123,200 square acres, and ranks in size the fourth district in the state. A political arrangement divides it into three parishes, viz. St. Bartholomew's, St. Paul's, and St. George's, Dorchester.

Colleton, lying between the districts of Charleston and Beaufort, possesses all the agricultural characteristics and advantages of these districts, except a sea coast; only one point of it being open to the ocean. The tides flow up its rivers for about thirty miles from the sea, and the water is salt about one third this distance. The soil of this district has been classed under three heads,—1st, The marsh or tide lands, which are adapted particularly to the culture of rice; 2d, the swamp lands which are equally rich, and planted mostly in cotton; and 3d, the high lands near them, which are chiefly valuable because of their timber. Portions of these uplands being found productive, are assigned to provision culture. The face of the country is flat and unimposing, but the rich foliage of the swamps, of all hues and shades of hue, the gigantic height and bulk of the trees, their great variety of form and appearance, greatly relieve the disadvantageous inferiority to the eye, which the uniform levels of the land around occasion. In its present physical state, the climate of Colleton district is unhealthy; but the sandy regions are places of retreat, in the upper parts of the district, to which the planters resort during the sickly months, with safety. The staple productions are rice and cotton. Its provision crops include potatoes and all varieties of grain. For its products, manufactures, &c. according to the census of 1840, see the table in the Appendix.

The rivers of Colleton are numerous and productive. Among the most important are, the Edisto, Combahee, Ashepoo, Stono, Salkehatchie and Ashley. The Combahee separates it from Beaufort. This river, and that of the Edisto, are navigable all their length in this district. A junction, by a canal only fourteen miles in length, of the Ashley and the Edisto, is a work which has been contemplated since 1765. It would save ninety miles of difficult and dangerous navigation, and prove of incalculable benefit to the districts of Charleston, Colleton, Barnwell and Orangeburg. The fish in these streams are numerous. Colleton, in this respect, shares the resources of Beaufort and Charleston; and the large blue cat of the Edisto, is famous all along the borders of that river.

The islands in the neighborhood of the sea are numerous, and some of them in a high state of cultivation. These are Slan's, Burden's, Ashe's, Warren's, Hutchinson's, Young's, &c. White Point is a fine prominence looking out upon the sea, at one of the mouths of the Edisto, which had been chosen as a place of settlement by successive colonists.

Colleton, lying within the alluvial region, possesses no other kind of stone, than that species of calcareous rock, called shell limestone; considerable quarries of which are found at different places. Marine shells are found every where, but no minerals.

The timber trees are in abundance, of the finest description. The pine of the Edisto supplies Charleston, and a considerable portion finds its way to the West Indies. Besides the pine, there are, the live oak, cypress, poplar, ash, hickory, beech, walnut, palmetto, and many others. Shingles of the cypress are very durable and greatly preferred over all other. Game is plentiful; the deer is numerous, and hunting clubs are proportionately so. The birds are such as are common to the neighboring districts.

The population of Colleton, by the census of 1840, is 25,548; of whom 6,302 are free, and 19,246 slaves. St. Paul's parish contains a total of 5,538, of which 751 are free white, 128 free colored, and 4,659 are slaves. St. George's parish contains a total of 4,188; of whom 1,577 are free white, 69 free colored, and 2,542 are slaves. St. Bartholomew's parish has a population of 15,884; of whom 3,548 are free white, 231 are free colored, and 12,105 are slaves. Colleton sends three senators, and six representatives to the state legislature.

Colleton district was named in honor of sir John Colleton, one of the lords proprietors of the province. Its chief town is Walterborough, which is the seat of justice for the district. It lies in a healthy region in St. Bartholomew's parish, and is a place of some trade, a place of resort for health, and altogether an attractive settlement. It is fifty miles from Charleston, and about ninety from the capital of the state. It has a handsome Court-House, three churches, a Library and Market House, two Academies, a Jail, and several fine dwellings. Summerville is a pleasant retreat during the sickly months. It lies in St. George's parish, is penetrated by the Hamburg rail-road, and is twenty-one miles from Charleston. During the summer, it contains from 300 to to 400 inhabitants. In winter, it is nearly abandoned.

Five miles to the south of it, are the ruins of the old town of Dorchester, on Ashley river, before and during the revolution, a place of considerable importance. Jacksonborough is a small town on the bank of the Edisto, occupying the site of Pon Pon, an ancient town of the Indians. The trade of this place was once considerable, and as the British power became broken, towards the close of the war of the revolution, and when their forces became confined to the immediate limits of Charleston, Jacksonborough became temporarily the seat of the state legislation. The legislature was convened here in 1782. Willtown is a small village, in St. Paul's parish, occupying a high bluff, on the margin of the Edisto, which was once the site of a strong fortress, built by the early colonists. The people of Willtown distinguished themselves in 1739, in putting down an insurrection of the negroes, which had been fomented by the Spaniards of Florida. For the particulars, see the History of South Carolina. Ashepoo, one of the earliest English inland settlements of the state, lies on the western branch of the river Ashepoo, in the parish of St. Bartholomew. It was desolated by the Indians, in the great insurrection of the Yemassees in 1715; but flourished again until the revolution. An Episcopal chapel, and a few dwellings, are all that remain.

Colleton has produced many eminent men, among whom we may especially mention, colonel Hayne, who was executed by the British; colonel Harden, a very gallant revolutionary officer, and major Snipes, whose achievements in the partisan warfare of the low countey, narrated by tradition, were distinguished by an audacity which reminds one very much of the heroism of the middle ages. Colleton has been the scene of many fierce and bloody battles. Near the bridge of Salkehatchie, they will shew you certain tumuli, which serve as memorials of the sanguinary and conclusive fight between governor Craven, and the Yemassees, under the chief Sanutee. In the same neighborhood, the American cavalry was surprised just after the fall of Charleston, and here colonel Harden fought one of his best battles with the English. On the banks of the Stono, you are again reminded of the bravery of governor Craven, who defeated in this place a large body of Florida Indians; and here also took place the battle of Stono, in 1777, when general Lincoln attacked the entrenchments of Prevost. Near Parker's ferry, you are reminded of one of the brilliant operations of Marion, which took place in 1781, and at the Tar Bluff, on the Combahee, you are shown the spot where the gallant Laurens perished, in a British ambush. The whole district is full of these un-interesting memorials, for the particulars of which the reader is referred to the History of South Carolina.

The wealthy classes of Colleton are usually well educated ; a large sum is appropriated to the poor schools, but the system is necessarily defective, in districts so sparsely settled, and where the climate is so unfavorable to health. The benefits derived from the free school fund are inconsiderable. In religious respects, there is gradual improvement ; the Methodist is the most numerous religious sect, and is most properly active in its work.

DARLINGTON DISTRICT.

The District of DARLINGTON was first settled in 1750, by emigrants from Virginia. Its name was probably derived from that of colonel Darlington, a favorite leader in the war of the revolution. Darlington lies within the alluvial region of the state. It is of compact form, having the great Pedee as a line on the north-east, by which river it is separated from Marlborough district; and Lynch's creek on the south-west, by which it is separated from Sumter; Cedar creek separates it on the north-west from Chesterfield; on the south-east it is bounded by Marion and a small portion of Williamsburg. It contains 576,000 acres, and is, on an average, thirty miles square.

The river lands of Darlington are of great fertility. The swamps of Pedee, Black river and Lynch's creek, are very rich, and the former are in some places from two to six miles in width. The intermediate lands are barren and inferior, but interspersed occasionally with good tracts of timber. The low lands of the Pedee yield the finest crops of corn and cotton. They are mostly secured from freshets by embankment. The lower, or south corner of Darlington, contains masses of the marine shell limestone. Metallic matter, resembling iron, is found among the shallows of the Pedee. It is employed for dyeing black, for which purpose it is preferred to copperas;—of this, there is great abundance.

The face of the country is undulatory; some of the hills rise into eminences more than three hundred feet above the ocean. In these parts the climate is healthy and pleasant; but along the water courses and rivers, during the autumn, fevers prevail.

Cotton is the chief marketable commodity. Grain is raised in sufficient quantities for home consumption.

The timber trees in the low lands are very large. The timber in the high lands is generally inferior. Among the forest trees are, the pine, the black and white oak, cypress, cotton-tree, sycamore, sweet gum, &c. The fruit trees are the peach, nectarine and cherry. The grape is abundant, and a very good domestic wine has been made from it. Game is not now in abundance. The deer and turkey are seldom met with. Partridges, doves, snipe and woodcock, are, however, in plenty; also, the wild duck, and occasionally wild geese and pigeons. The singing birds are the mock-bird, thrush, red-bird, and blue-bird.

Darlington is a well watered district. The Pedee has a good steamboat navigation its whole length. Black creek is navigable thirty miles from its junction with the Pedee; and Lynch's creek, eighty miles from where it joins the same river. By removing some obstructions, it may be made navigable into Chesterfield. There are numerous other streams of value and importance,—such as Sparrow creek, Jeffery's creek, Cedar, Swift, Highhill, Buckholt's, Alligator, Black Swamp, Lake Swamp, Middle Swamp, &c. On the Pedee there are excellent fisheries for shad and sturgeon, in which quantities are caught. The herring, also, visits this river. There are, also, the trout, the bream, catfish, &c.

The population of Darlington, by the census of 1840, is 14,822, of whom 7,560 are slaves. The district is entitled to one senator, and two representatives in the legislature of the state.

Education has not been left unattended to in Darlington. The schools are frequent and flourishing. Free schools are numerous, and an annual appropriation of six hundred dollars is made by the state for their support. The Baptist is the most numerous religious sect in the district—next to it, the Methodist and Presbyterian. Some attention has been paid to manufactures, confined however to the coarser stuffs; but this branch of industry does not flourish, people preferring to raise the raw material, rather than to make it into cloth.

The village of Darlington, situated on Swift creek, is the seat of justice for the district. It is a small but neat town, containing a handsome Court House of brick, a Jail, sundry taverns, &c. It lies seventy-five miles from Columbia and one hundred and thirty from Charleston.

Darlington has three other villages, which are places of summer retreat. The principal of these is Society Hill, a rural eminence, houses and trees interspersed picturesquely, and without any regard to order. It promises to be a place of equal beauty and importance, needing but a little more attention to the style of building, and a little more order in arrangement for the former. Its population is about 600. Well placed for health and having many facilities for trade, its promise of increase and prosperity appears well founded. It contains churches for the Baptist and Methodist persuasions, and has a good Academy. Two or more steamboats, and other vessels, ply between it and Georgetown. Society Hill was once called Greenville.

Old Cheraw was once the seat of justice for a large district of the same name. But it has long been since abandoned. Two other villages, Springville and Mechanicsville, are chiefly valuable for the security for health which they afford. They are places of residence chiefly during the summer season.

Cheraw is the only Indian name preserved in this district.

EDGEFIELD DISTRICT.

The District of EDGEFIELD was settled chiefly by emigrants from Virginia and North Carolina. Its name is presumed to have been derived from its geographical position, on the edge of the state, and adjoining the state of Georgia. Edgefield lies on the south-west border of the state, bounded in this quarter by the Savannah river, which separates it from Georgia. On the east and southeast, it is bounded by Lexington, Orangeburg and Barnwell districts; on the north and east, by the Saluda, which separates it from Newberry; and on the northwest by Abbeville. The average length of the district is forty-six miles; breadth thirty-seven. It contains 1,089,280 acres, and is the fifth district, in point of size, in the state.

The soil of Edgefield is generally good, and partakes of several varieties. A portion of it, in the eastern and southern parts of the district, is sandy, bearing the long-leaved pine, such as belongs to the country along the seaboard; the rest is the oak and hickory land, such as belongs to mountain regions. This latter portion yields good crops, is of rich quality; of various colors, red, white and black; of sand and loam, with clay foundation. The face of this part of the country of Edgefield is very hilly, and this constitutes the only objection to the soil in an agricultural point of view. It is liable to wash into gullies in heavy rains. The productions are such as are raised generally in the middle and upper country,—cotton and corn, and grain of every description. The pine lands are peculiarly adapted to the cultivation of peas, beans and potatoes. The oak and hickory lands yield wheat, tobacco, corn, hemp, cotton, &c. The timber trees of Edgefield are, pine, (long and short leaf,) oak, hickory, elm, ash, gum, &c. The fruit trees are, apple, peach, plum, cherry, pear, quince, &c. The birds are, the turtle-dove, mocking-bird, partridge, robin, wren, snow-bird, red-bird, swallow, wood-pecker, woodcock, buzzard, hawk, owl, &c. In the upper division of the district, there are considerable bodies of granite, and quarries of excellent freestone, suitable for millstones. Beds of iron ore have been discovered in different places.

The chief navigable stream in Edgefield, is the Savannah, which is navigable for steamboats from Hamburg to Charleston; and for smaller craft, above, to Vienna, in South Carolina, and Petersburg in Georgia. The Saluda is next in importance, and is navigable for boats carrying fifty bales of cotton, the whole length of the district. The Sapona, or Steven's creek, which empties into the Savannah, might, according to Mills, be made navigable into the heart of the district. Shaw's creek, Little Saluda, and some other smaller streams, might, it is supposed, by a small amount of labor, be converted into navigable courses of considerable value. The Seraw, Serannah, and Cussaboe, are streams originally with musical Indian names, which are made to yield to such vulgar appellations as Horse creek, Cuffytown creek, Hardlabor creek, &c. The principal fish are, shad, (during spring,) cat, perch, rock, pike, trout, red-horse, &c. The average value of land in Edgefield is probably $2,50 per acre. The agriculture of the district, like that of most parts of the state, is improving. Manuring is becoming a system, and will become more so, in the diminished value of cotton as a product. Hamburg, Augusta and Charleston, are the principal markets. The climate of Edgefield is mild, and generally speaking, healthy. The diseases are of a bilious kind, and occur chiefly on the mill seats, and near the banks of creeks and rivers.

The population of Edgefield, by the census of 1840, is 32,853; of these 15,315 are free; the rest slaves. She is entitled to one senator and six representatives in the legislature of the state. The principal occupation of the people is agriculture. The chief towns are Hamburg and Edgefield. The former is a flourishing trading town on the north-east bank of Savannah river, opposite the city of Augusta in Georgia, and a competitor for a considerable portion of its trade. It is the *terminus* of the Charleston and Hamburg rail road; and, with this facility, and a steamboat communication with Charleston and Savannah, by the Savannah river, it lacks, perhaps, nothing but capital to render it a formidable rival of its Georgia neighbor. It is distant from Charleston, by rail road, one hundred and thirty-six miles; twenty-three south of Edgefield; and contains a population of about 1,500. Its trade is chiefly in cotton, corn and tobacco.

The court town bears the name of the district. It is a neat and thriving village, on elevated ground, lying in the head fork of Beaver Dam creek. It contains a population of five six or hundred; has a neat Court House and Church, numerous fine dwelling houses, and issues an interesting weekly newspaper. The situation of Edgefield village, is one of uninterrupted health, lying upon the ridge which separates the pine and oak lands, between the waters of Edisto, Savannah and Saluda. It is sixty-two miles from Columbia, and one hundred and fifty-seven from Charleston.

Pottersville is a small village, about a mile and a half from Edgefield, chiefly distinguished by its pottery, in which stone ware of a superior kind has been extensively manufactured, and may be to an incomputable extent. Other potteries are also to be found in this district. At Pottersville there is a cotton factory, for the manufacture of the coarser fabrics.

Richardsonville is another small village, seventeen miles north of the court house. Fort Moore, five miles south-east from Hamburg, is the site of an old fortress and place of settlement. It was first occupied in 1740.

Education and morals, in Edgefield, have undergone great improvement within a few years. She is strong in her intellectual men, who exercise a salutary influence over civilization. Religion is benevolent and active; her schools are good, and the subject of education is beginning to make itself felt in its proper force every where. There are several academies and numerous private schools. Fifteen hundred to two thousand dollars are annually appropriated to the free schools by the state legislature. The religious denominations are chiefly Baptist and Methodist. An Agricultural Society, which promises to be active and of great value, has recently been established. There is little real poverty in Edgefield.

Edgefield district was once a part of the vast possessions of the Muscoghee nation. It has been the scene of frequent warfare since their day; and has produced several eminent men, among whom may be named, colonel Le Roy Hammond, a distinguished leader against the Indians, before and during the war of the revolution; captain Thomas Harvey, who acquired credit in the Cherokee war, and was slain in battle by the tories, after having won the victory. Major Hugh Middleton, colonel Purvis, captains Ryan and Butler, were also men of rank, and well remembered for their Indian and revolutionary valor. This list might be numerously extended, were this the place for it. For the achievements in this quarter, see the History of the State.

FAIRFIELD DISTRICT.

FAIRFIELD was first settled by emigrants from Virginia and North Carolina. It derives its name, most probably, from the grateful appearance which it made, in the eyes of wanderers, weary with long looking for a resting place. It is bounded, on the north by Chester district; on the south by Richland; on the west and south-west by Broad river, which divides it from Union, Newberry and Lexington; south-west by Lexington; and on the north-east, by the Wateree and Catawba rivers, which separate it from a part of Lancaster and Kershaw. Fairfield is, on an average, thirty-two miles in length, twenty-three in width, and contains about 471,040 square acres.

With the exception of a slip of sandy pine land, on its south-eastern limit, Fairfield is within the granite region. In its general aspect, the country is much diversified, justifying its name, lying now in level plains, rising into slopes and gentle undulations, and sometimes swelling into rugged surface and imposing mountain. The soil is very various, combining the best and worst of the upper country. The lands on the water courses are rich and inexhaustible; the uplands are perhaps too hilly for safe cultivation in a season of much rain. Cotton, of the short staple, is much cultivated; the small grains grow well in Fairfield; corn and wheat in particular. Of these, with rye, oats, barley and potatoes, the crops are usually abundant.

The chief rivers are the Broad, or Eswawpuddenah, which is navigable the whole length of the district; as also the Catawba and Wateree, (which, being one river, becomes, in this district, one in name also.) Little river, which empties into the Broad, is only partially navigable. It has numerous branches, and is a stream of much importance. Wateree creek, the entrance of which, into the Catawba, imposes upon the latter its name, is the next considerable stream. This union takes place three and a half miles above the line of Lancaster and Kershaw. The lands on the banks of this stream are noted for their fertility. Dutchman's creek, which empties into the Wateree; and Beaver, which empties into Broad river; are both valuable; the one being a creek, the other a beautiful stream; noted, also, as the first place of white settlement in the district. There are other streams,—the Suwannee, Rocky, Morris, Fox, Bear, &c. which find their way into the Wateree. The tributaries of the Broad, in Fairfield, are Wilkinson, Terrible, Rock, Goodacon, and Cool Branch. In these two main rivers, the Broad and Wateree, are numerous islands, all fertile and some of them in cultivation.

The fish are, the shad and sturgeon, the trout, pike, perch, eel, gar, red-horse, suck, carp, &c.

Fairfield has the finest granite for building; soapstone, sandstone, slatestone, gneiss and hornblende, are occasionally to be seen. A remarkably high rock, on the road from Columbia, and four miles from Winnsboro, is called, from its appearance, the Anvil rock. Rock crystals are common; also, crystalized quartz; iron is abundant, and pyrites. A valuable mineral spring, good in dyspeptic and cutaneous diseases, is found within ten miles of Winnsboro.

The forests of Fairfield contain the finest timber and in great variety; among which are, the poplar, hickory, walnut, pine, beech, birch, oak, (black, white and red, Spanish, post and Turkey,) ash, elm, linden, gum, sugar, maple, cherry, dogwood, sassafras, papaw, iron wood, cotton, cedar, &c. The wild fruit trees are, crab-apple, chinquapin, mulberry, persimmon, haw, hazelnut, walnut, hickory-nut, cherry, chestnut, &c. The cultivated fruit trees, are, peach, quince, apple, pear, apricot, fig, pomegranate, cherry, plum, almond, &c.

The shrub and bush fruits are, strawberry, raspberry, whortleberry, gooseberry, &c.

The game are, deer, turkey, foxes, raccoons, opossums, squirrels, &c. Of birds, migratory and domestic, there are, the martin, swallow, duck, snow-bird, robin, mock-bird, cat-bird, humming-bird, snipe, wood-pecker, whippoorwill, plover, kingfisher, &c.; jay, red-bird and sparrow; turkey, partridge, dove, woodcock, crow, owl, hawk and black-bird. The wild pigeon occasionally appears, and sometimes the bald eagle.

The population of Fairfield, by the census of 1840, is 20,165; of these, 7,660 are free; 12,505 slaves. The district is entitled to one senator and four representatives in the legislature of the state. The employments of the people are chiefly agricultural; domestic manufactures are carried on to considerable extent. The water courses furnish numerous mill seats, but these works are chiefly used for sawing lumber, ginning cotton, or grinding corn.

Winnsboro is the seat of justice, and the town of most importance in the district. It is a healthy and pleasant spot, thirty miles from Columbia, and one hundred and fifty from Charleston. It is placed on the dividing ridge between the rivers Wateree and Broad. A main branch of the Wateree creek heads near the village. This and other streams furnish excellent springs of water. The town stands on an elevation of more than three hundred feet above the Wateree river, and about five hundred feet above the ocean. The lands around are fertile, undulating and greatly improved. The population is near 500. It has a handsome Court House and Jail, an Academy, three Churches, a Masonic Hall and Markethouse. Mount Zion college was established here prior to the revolution, and received a charter in 1777. Some of the dwellings in Winnsboro, are handsomely built. In 1780, lord Cornwallis made this village his head quarters. The cotton gins manufactured in Winnsboro, have a high reputation throughout the state. There are some other villages in the district. Monticello, lying between Little river and Wilkinson's creek, contains an Academy, a few houses, and occupies in the center of a healthy, rich and populous neighborhood. Rocky Mount, or Grimkeville, stands on the Catawba river, of which it commands a beautiful view; and Longtown, situate on a high sand ridge, twenty miles east of Winnsboro, is the resort of the planters of the Wateree during the autumn season.

This district lies in a salubrious region. The climate is pleasant and healthy. Fevers occur in the fall, along the rich bottoms and the water courses; but there are few portions of the upper country more healthy than this. The instances of longevity are numerous.

A considerate regard is paid to education in Fairfield. The academies and schools are numerous. The free schools receive twelve hundred dollars from the state annually. A decent sense of religious duty is prevalent, and Sunday schools are efficiently exercised. The religious sects are Presbyterian, Methodist, Baptist, Episcopalian and Dutch Reformed. Fairfield is prominent, indeed, for its high sense of religious and moral obligation. It has also made some advance in literature, and there are many excellent private libraries.

The territory of Fairfield was once a part of the heritage of the Catawbas. They received the whites kindly, and were affectionately true to them through all periods.

Fairfield has furnished to the state her full share of distinguished men. Among these were general Richard Winn, who was a prominent leader in the revolutionary war. Thomas Woodward has the reputation of having instituted the sort of forest-justice—in the absence of regular laws and officers—which went by the name of *regulation*. He is claimed to have been the *first regulator*.

GEORGETOWN DISTRICT.

GEORGETOWN lies upon the Atlantic, to which it presents a considerable front, and from which it is separated by a sand ridge and chain of islands. It is bounded on the south-west by Santee river; which separates it from Charleston district; on the north-west by Williamsburg; on the north-east by a part of Marion district; on the east by the Great Pedee, and Horry district, and on the south-east by the Atlantic ocean. The length of the district averages thirty-eight miles; breadth twenty-four; and includes 583,680 acres.

The islands are Bull, Waccana, North, Santee, Cat, Sandy, Crow, &c.

The inlets, along the coast, are North, Georgetown, Gahany, North and South Santee, and the bay of Winyaw. The rivers are the Great Pedee; Waccamaw, Weenee, or Black, Sampit, North and South Santee; all of which are navigable, wherever they traverse the district. The face of the country is uniformly flat and unimproving. The river lands are a deep rich mould of inexhaustible fertility; next to these are the inland swamps; the pine ridges are little else than sand, bottomed sometimes on clay, and having occasionally a productive soil. The tide lands, which constitute the famous rice lands, are the most valuable in the district. The fertile regions are appropriated almost exclusively to rice, which is produced in great abundance. After rice, cotton is the next great product. But little corn is raised. The other products, though in small quantities, are potatoes, wheat, oats, &c. Among the exports are, tar, pitch and turpentine, staves, &c.

The pine is the most common tree of this district. The river swamps abound in cypress, and their margins with the various kinds of oak, hickory, poplar, ash, chestnut, cedar, beech, sycamore, laurel, cotton-tree, &c. The live-oak, near the sea, is large and abundant.

The fruits are, the peach, plum, apricot, fig, cherry, nectarine, orange, pomegranate, grape, &c. The woods abound with fragrant trees, shrubs and vines,—the magnolia, yellow jessamine, eglantine, bay, honey-suckle, azalea, vanilla, asters, lilies, wild rose, &c.

The waters teem with the finest fish, both of the salt and fresh water tribes—the shad and herring in spring; the trout, pike, bream, perch, sturgeon, rock, terrapin, soft shelled turtle, carp, &c.; the drum, bass, sheep's-head, mullet, cavalli, whiting, black; oysters, crabs, sea-turtle, shrimps, &c.

Of game there is plenty; deer, foxes, rabbits, raccoons, and occasionally the wolf and bear. Of birds, the turkey, goose, duck, (of all varieties,) snipe, woodcock and pigeon; partridge, plover and rice-bird; eagle, hawk, owl; black-bird, mocking-bird and bullfinch. Snakes are numerous in swamp and forest; and the alligator, in fresh, tide and brackish waters, grows to an enormous size.

The climate is moist, hot and unhealthy; subject to fevers in summer and agues in autumn. There are choice spots however, along the sea shore, to which the inhabitants resort for health; among these is North, and the neighboring islands.

The population of Georgetown district, by the census of 1840, is 18,274; of these, 2,281 are free; the rest are slaves. The district comprises two parishes, viz.—All-Saints and Prince George, each of which is entitled to a senator in the state legislature, where the district has four representatives.

Agriculture is the only employment. There are no manufactures. A small portion of the free population is engaged in trade. There are few native schools, the planters generally preferring that their children should be educated in healthier districts. The free schools are moderately attended. The state appropriates to this object, twelve hundred dollars per annum.

Georgetown is the seat of justice for the district. It is situated on the north side of the river Sampit, near its junction with Winyaw bay, and, in a straight line, about nine miles from the sea. Vessels of considerable size may approach the town and lie at the wharves. Georgetown is well situated for trade, surrounded by fertile and cultivated lands close to the sea, with a safe harbor and an extensive back country. It contains about 1500 inhabitants, has a handsome Court House, a Bank, Jail, Market place, and several churches. There is a public Library, and several private societies; among which is the the Winyaw Indigo Society, incorporated in 1756, which maintains a school of twenty-five orphan children, and has a funded capital of thirty thousand dollars. Georgetown has an Agricultural Society also, and issues two weekly newspapers.

The climate of Georgetown, however, is so sickly as to impair most of its advantages as a place of trade. Its trade is chiefly carried on through and with Charleston, from which it is distant 61 miles. It is distant from Columbia 121 miles. La Grange, on North island, the summer retreat of the people of Georgetown, is noted as the spot where La Fayette first landed in America, during the revolution. It is a delightful and salubrious residence. Georgetown has been the seat of much interesting occurrence, particularly during the revolutionary war. In its neighborhood are shown the frequent scenes of Marion's achievements. It was twice attacked by him, while it lay in possession of the British, and at last captured. The district is full of such memorials. It has produced several distinguished men, among whom may be mentioned the great historical painter, Washington Allston.

GREENVILLE DISTRICT.

The District of GREENVILLE received its first settlers in 1766, from Virginia and Pennsylvania; but the progress of settlement was slow until the close of the Cherokee war. The face of the country, verdant and picturesque, is supposed to have led to the adoption of its name. The Cherokees were the original possessors of the soil.

Greenville is bounded on the north by North Carolina; on the east and south by the districts of Spartanburg and Laurens; west by the Saluda river, which divides it from Pendleton. Its extreme length, from north to south, is fifty miles; its average breadth does not exceed twenty. It contains about 414,720 square acres. The country is elevated; in the south, undulating and attractive; in the north, mountainous and imposing. The soil is various, embracing sand, clay, gravel, and stone. Much of it, properly cultivated, is capable of yielding bountiful returns to the hands of industry. It is well adapted to the culture of all the small grains, and corn, tobacco, and green seed cotton.

The climate is one of the most delightful in the world; the diseases are few; the lands are well drained and irrigated, and the mountains are admirable barriers against the chilling blasts of winter.

Rocks of granite, gneiss, quartz, &c. are found in great abundance; minerals of several kinds have been discovered—iron, yellow ochre, pyrites, lead ore, the emerald, and many others. The chief materials for building are rock and clay. Materials of wood are neither very good nor in great quantity.

The timber trees are, the short-leaved pine, poplar, chestnut, white, red, and Spanish oak, maple, walnut and cherry. The fruit trees are the apple, quince, plum, &c.

Greenville, though finely watered, does not possess many navigable facilities. The Saluda and Tyger rivers are interrupted by rocks and falls of considerable extent. The Reedy river, which flows through the district, and passes by the court house, it is thought might be made useful, by canals, for the purpose of communicating with the Saluda, and thus open a communication by water with Columbia, and thence to Charleston. The other chief river is the Enoree. There are several branches of the Saluda, and numerous smaller streams. In these streams fish of various kinds are caught,—such as the trout, rock, red-horse, &c. The birds of Greenville are such as are common to all the upper districts.

Greenville, to the north, is walled in by the mountain barriers of the Blue Ridge, some of the spurs from which make into the very heart of the district. Such is Paris mountain. Other mountains within its limits are called, the Hogback, Glassy, Cæsar's Head, Dismal, Prospect and Pine. The Hogback is steep, difficult of ascent and dangerous. Its name is derived from its appearance. On the top of the mountain is the Cold Spring, perpetually gushing forth, and the abandoned plantation of a hermit. The Glassy mountain, which adjoins the Hogback, is so named because the water, trickling down its sides, and frozen in winter, reflects the blaze of the sun with the dazzling lustre of a mirror. Cæsar's Head and Dismal mountains are abrupt and highly picturesque eminences. The former, indeed, though little known, is described as presenting one of the most beautiful prospects in America.

The population of Greenville, by the census of 1840, is 17,839; of whom 12,534 are free, and 5,305 slaves. It is entitled to one senator and four representatives in the state legislature. Agriculture constitutes the chief employment of the people. The manufactures are for purely domestic objects. There have been several iron works on the Reedy river which are now abandoned; but the working of iron, on a limited scale, still continues in different parts of the district.

GREENVILLE DISTRICT.

The people of Greenville have been honorably regardful of education and morals. The academies and schools are numerous and efficient. An appropriation of a thousand dollars per annum, for the free schools, is made by the legislature. The religious denominations are, Presbyterian, Methodist, Baptist and Episcopalian; the first named being the most numerous.

The village of Greenville is the seat of justice for the district. It is beautifully situated on a gentle and undulated plane. The Reedy river runs beside it, precipitating itself, in the immediate neighborhood, in a beautiful cascade, over an immense bed of rocks, The Paris mountain, at a distance of seven miles, presents another object similarly picturesque, for the admirer of fine scenery. The village is regularly laid out in squares, and, equally grateful to health and sight, is preferred as a place of resort. The public buildings are a handsome brick Court House, a Jail, two or three houses of public worship, a male and female Academy, several public houses of great size, and many private residences which are equally handsome and spacious. The population is estimated at 8 or 900. There is a public Library, a weekly and well conducted newspaper, and an Agricultural Society. Greenville is 108 miles from Columbia, and 225 from Charleston. The district has given birth to several distinguished men. It is destined, from the salubrity of its climate, its fertility of soil, and beauty of situation, to cherish a population as numerous as it is now vigorous and virtuous.

HORRY DISTRICT.

The District of HORRY was principally settled by Irish emigrants in 1733. It receives its name from general Horry of revolutionary renown. Horry forms the north-eastern corner of the state and fronts on the ocean, which bounds it on the south-east for a space of thirty-one miles. On the north-east it is bounded by North Carolina; on the south by Georgetown; north-east by Georgetown and Marion, and north-west by the latter. Its average length is thirty-seven miles; breadth twenty-nine. It contains about 687,720 acres.

The face of the country is uniformly flat; along the rivers the soil is rich and highly productive. The uplands are of light soil, with a clay basis. But the waste lands are very extensive, and the river lands require to be reclaimed for cultivation. Cotton, corn and rice are the chief productions. Wheat, peas and potatoes are raised in abundant quantities for domestic use. Lumber, tar and turpentine are among the exports. Cloths of domestic manufacture are considerably used.

Horry is a well watered district. With a front upon the sea of thirty miles, it has yet a number of lakes and streams. Of the former are, Kingston, Lake Swamp, &c. The rivers are, the Great and Little Pedee; the former navigable for vessels of sixty tons, and the latter for boats drawing three feet water, up to the North Carolina line. The Waccamaw is navigable for vessels of one hundred tons above Conwayborough, subject to the obstruction of one sand shoal, which, at low water, has a depth of six feet. There are also Lumber and Little river, and several smaller streams. Bull creek is also navigable for large vessels. Horry maintains, in navigation, fifteen or twenty vessels, and employs from eighty to one hundred seamen.

The waters abound in fish, among which are, the trout, bream, jack, perch, shad, and (in season) the herring. Besides these, there are the usual sea-fish.

The forest trees are, the long-leaved pine, the cypress and oak, (live and white, &c.) The fruit trees are, the peach, apple, pear, plum, fig and cherry. The game are, deer, turkey, duck, (various kinds,) fox, wild-cat, and, occasionally, the bear. Of birds there are, the partridge, dove, &c. Compact shell limestone is found on the Waccamaw. Lime is prepared from oyster shells.

The population of Horry, according to the census of 1840, is 5,755; of these, 4,181 are free; 1,574 slaves. It is entitled to one senator and one representative in the state legistature. The population has suffered much from emigration. The climate, particularly along the sea, is favorable to health. In the neighborhood of the creeks, rivers and swamps, agues and fevers prevail during the months of autumn.

Kingston, or Conwayborough, is the seat of justice for the district. It lies on the west side of the river Waccamaw, at its junction with the lake of the same name. It is distant from Charleston 117, and from Columbia, 135 miles. It is a place of small population and trade. The residents are scarce 200. Its chief importance is due to its being the district town. Kingston lake is a fine sheet of water. There is another small settlement, established chiefly with reference to trade, is placed upon Little river, a few miles from the sea. Its exports, in tar, pitch and lumber, are considerable.

The Baptists are the most numerous religious sect in Horry; after them, the Methodists, the Presbyterians and Episcopalians. Education is improving. The people are generally moral and religious in their habits. There are few paupers. The legislature appropriates annually five or six hundred dollars for the free schools.

This district gave birth to many distinguished whigs of the revolution. It was the theatre of much fierce fighting between the whigs and tories. Bear Bluff, on Waccamaw river, is pointed out as the scene of one of these conflicts.

KERSHAW DISTRICT.

The first settlement of KERSHAW was made by a colony of Irish Quakers, about the year 1750. The district takes its name from colonel Joseph Kershaw, an officer of great local reputation, during and previous to the war of the revolution.

Kershaw is bounded on the north-east by Sumter; on the north-west by Richland; on the west and north by Fairfield; on the north-west and north by Lancaster; on the north-east by Chesterfield and Darlington, from which it is separated by Big Lynch's creek. The average length of the district is about thirty-two miles; width twenty-seven; number of acres, about 553,000.

Kershaw lies immediately between the primitive and alluvial formation. The lower line of the granite region runs through the middle of the district. The sand hills are high and barren. The face of the country is varied and agreeable. It contains every variety of soil,—very rich and very inferior. The rivers have great extent of alluvial low grounds, easy of reclamation, generally above the influence of freshets. In the upper parts of the districts, clay lands are found; but the great body of uplands are usually sandy. Numerous streams irrigate the highlands, and furnish many choice spots for the cultivator.

The climate is pleasant and commonly healthy, except in the neighborhood of rivers. The products of the soil are, cotton, corn, wheat, rye, oats, &c. Cotton is raised for export; all the rest for home consumption. Domestic manufacturing establishments are large and numerous. Flour has been manufactured for sale to a considerable amount, but has been superseded by cotton. So, also, from the palma christi, was cold pressed oil once made, at the rate of one hundred and fifty gallons to the acre. That, too, has been abandoned for cotton.

The Wateree and Kaddipah (or Lynch's) are navigable streams. There are other rivers of importance, viz. Little Lynch's, Flat Rock, Hanging Rock, Beaver, Sanders, Pine Tree, &c. Fine fish are afforded by most of these waters.

Kershaw has several mineral springs which have considerable domestic reputation. Among these, the most important are those at Liberty Hill. A gold mine has been worked on Little Lynch's creek, on the Lancaster boundary line, which proved to be one of the richest in the south.

The population of Kershaw, by the census of 1840, is 12,281. Of these, 4,238 are free, and 8,043 slaves. Kershaw is entitled to one senator and two representatives in the state legislature. One thousand dollars is the state annual appropriation for the free schools of the district.

The chief interest of Kershaw centres in and about the town of Camden. This place has been particularly famous from the war of the revolution. Camden is the seat of justice for the district, and is the oldest inland town of the state, being settled in 1750. It is handsomely situated on a plain, on the east bank of the Wateree river, about a mile from it, and at an elevation above it of nearly one hundred feet. It is almost an island. Pine Tree creek, with Belton's Branch, sweeping round three sides, and, by their head springs, nearly meeting on the fourth. The town limits embrace, from east to west, one mile; and in length, from south to north, nearly two. It was laid out in squares in 1760, chartered in 1769, had a regular police and was thriving before the revolution. That event proved for a time fatal to its prosperity. It fell into the hands of the British, was made a fortified town, and destroyed by them when they were compelled to abandon it. For the interesting incidents connected with its fortunes, see the History of South Carolina. Here, in this neighborhood, Cornwallis defeated Gates; De

Kalb was slain; Rawdon and Greene met in a memorable but drawn battle; and colonel Washington, by a happy *ruse de guerre*, captured Rugely. Camden is now a beautiful and flourishing town, and carries on a considerable trade with Charleston, from which it is distant 130 miles. It is 33 miles from Columbia. It has also a considerable trade with the interior. Its population is about 2,300. It contains an elegant Court House, of superior classical design, a Jail, City Hall, Bank, public Library, several places of public worship, some of which are in the most graceful style of art; academies, schools, societies, and issues a neat weekly newspaper. Here, also, may be seen a graceful monument, raised by the gratitude of the citizens, to the memory of the brave old German, DeKalb, who perished at the head of the continentals, in the fatal battle at Gum Swamp, between Gates and Cornwallis. Camden suffered terribly, during the war, from British and tory atrocities. Kershaw has given to the state many distinguished citizens.

LANCASTER DISTRICT.

The first settlers in this district came from Pennsylvania and Virginia, about the year 1745, and planted their colony on the Waxhaw creek, in the immediate neighborhood of the Catawba Indians, then one of the most powerful Indian nations of the south. The name of the district was conferred upon it by the settlers from Pennsylvania, who came from Lancaster in that state.

Lancaster constitutes one part of the northern boundary of the state, and is placed entirely within the granite region. It is bounded on the west by the Catawba river, which divides it from York, Chester, and a part of Fairfield; on the south by Kershaw; on the north-east and north by the state of North Carolina and the district of Chesterfield. Lancaster is of irregular form; in its greatest length it is forty miles; width twenty-eight. It is computed to contain about 383,000 acres.

The face of Lancaster district is pleasingly varied by hill and dale, gentle undulation, rock and valley. The soil is equally various, comprising all sorts, from the sterile sand to the rich and fruitful loam. The rocks are mostly granite and white flint. Some beautiful quarries of white granite have been worked to advantage, and employed in many important and permanent structures. Slate and the asbestos, are said to lie along the Kaddipah, or Lynch's creek.

The Catawba river bounds this district on its longest side, and with some labor may be rendered navigable. So may Cain creek, Sugar creek, the Kaddipah, Twelve Mile creek, &c. The other streams by which this district is well watered are, the Waxhaw, Cane, Camp, Cedar, Hanging Rock, Tuckahoe, Little Lynch's, Flat and Wild Cat. The Catawba abounds in shad, when in season. The native fish are, the trout, rock, red-horse, perch, &c. In this river are several islands, viz. Patton, Davy, Taylor, Lackey, Mountain, Allen and Montgomery. Mountain island is the largest, and nearly two miles in length.

The Great Falls of the Catawba present a noble and imposing spectacle of great natural magnificence. The stream is gradually enclosed by rocks, straightened suddenly into a channel one third its width, and breaking from its prison with measureless violence, plunges headlong over its barriers of stone, from rock to rock, till it subsides in a basin nearly one hundred and fifty feet below.

Curiosities of this kind, though inferior in grandeur and beauty, are frequent in this district. Hanging Rock, Flat Rock, and Anvil Rock, are objects of particular interest and attraction, from their peculiar appearance, as well as from the events which distinguish them in history. Hanging Rock is the site of one of Sumter's famous battle grounds. It is of curious shape. Flat Rock is a mighty mass, five hundred yards across, composed of a very closely cemented and hard gravel. Its name is derived from its level surface, which is covered with numerous pits or cisterns, hollowed out, as supposed, by the Indians, for the purpose of holding water. The Anvil Rock is small, and would attract no notice, but for its shape. A mile from Hanging Rock there is a a mineral spring. Its waters act as a gentle aperient, and are strongly diuretic. It is beautifully situated, delightfully shaded, at the foot of a gentle descent, and has a fall for a *douche*, or shower bath. In process of time it will doubtless be a place of much resort for the invalid and idler.

The forest trees are, oak, pine, poplar, hickory, chestnut, ash, beech, sycamore, dogwood, walnut, sassafras, &c. The sugar-tree sometimes grows to a prodigious size.

The fruits are, apples, pears, peaches and cherries; grapes, berries of various kinds, chestnuts, walnuts, hickory nuts &c. The vine has occasionally been cultivated here with success. There are a few deer, wild turkeys, pigeons, ducks and geese, besides partridges, doves and woodcocks. Lancaster has also such other birds as are common to the country.

The climate of the country is bland and agreeable. Autumnal diseases prevail along the large water courses; but elsewhere the inhabitants enjoy excellent health, and instances of longevity are frequent.

Agriculture is the chief business of the people. The staple production is cotton, which finds its way, chiefly by land carriages, to Camden or Charleston. The other products are, corn, wheat, oats and rye, chiefly for home consumption. No goods are manufactured except for domestic use.

The population of Lancaster, by the census of 1840, is 9,907. Of these, 5,672 are free, and 4,235 are slaves. This district is one which suffered most from the emigration of its people to the south and west. Its population shows a repeated decrease, with each census, for the last twenty years. Entitled, in the state legislature, to one senator and two representatives.

The seat of justice derives its name from the district. Lancasterville was laid out in 1801, and has a present population of 4 or 500. It has some trade, and is comparatively prosperous. The town is regularly laid out. It is six miles from the Catawba river, fifty-nine from Columbia, and one hundred and seventy-six from Charleston. Its Court House and Jail are highly ornamented fabrics, and built of stone. The "Franklin Academy," a well endowed institution, has a handsome brick building. There are one or two other small villages in the district, such as Kingsbury; but they are not increasing. Of late, agriculture and education are regarded with a more just consideration than formerly. The state appropriates from twelve to fifteen hundred dollars to the free schools of the district, and several hundred poor children receive its benefit. Private schools are increasing and improving. The religious denominations are, Seceders, Presbyterians, Methodists, and a few Baptists.

Among the eminent men to whom this district has given birth, is Andrew Jackson, who was born on the waters of the Waxhaw, and seems to have been destined from the beginning to distinction. The Waxhaws were a nation of people expelled by the Catawbas. Lancaster was the scene of several battles during the revolution, the chief of which are, the battles of Hanging Rock, and Tarleton's massacre of Buford's command. For these interesting events see the History of the State.

LAURENS DISTRICT.

Laurens was settled about 1755, by a few emigrants from Virginia and Pennsylvania. The terror of the Indians, inspired by the defeat of Braddock, drove the borderers of Virginia, Pennsylvania and Maryland, to this and other more secure regions. The acquisition of the Cherokee country, to which nation the territory of Laurens originally belonged, under governor Glenn, of South Carolina, added still further to the population of the district. Its name was given in honor of Henry Laurens, one of the most eminent of the revolutionary patriots.

Laurens is situated about the middle of the upper country. It is bounded on the south-west by the Saluda river, which separates it from Abbeville; on the north-east by the Enoree, which divides it from Union and Spartanburg; on the north-west by Greenville; and on the south-east by Newberry. Its average length is thirty miles; its breadth twenty-four. It contains 560,800 square acres.

This district lies in the granite region. The face of the country is hilly. Granite is found in abundance; but no freestone or limestone. The soil is mostly clay and gravel; but it is productive, and well adapted to the culture of cotton, corn, wheat, tobacco, &c. Cotton is the only commodity raised for market. The manufactures are purely domestic.

The climate is temperate and very healthy. The atmosphere soft and serene. The soil is dry and elevated. Agues and fevers prevail to a small extent, during the autumn, in low, moist situations; particularly along the water courses.

The rivers are, the Saluda, Enoree, Little, and two arms of the Reedy river, which are remarkable, for running, at short intervals, nearly a parallel course with the Saluda and with each other. The Saluda is navigable by boats carrying seventy bales of cotton. The Enoree is a fine stream, and may be made navigable also. The smaller streams are, Duncan, Dunbar, Warrior, Indian, Bush and Raeburn. The fish are, trout, pike, carp, eel, suck, red-horse, perch and cat.

Laurens is a well timbered district. Besides the pine, of which there are both the long and short-leaved, there are numerous varieties of oak. The other trees are, poplar, chestnut, beech, dogwood, hickory, linden, locust, &c. The fruits are, apple and peach, (numerous kinds,) grape in abundance, plums, chinquapins, chestnuts, and various berries.

The game is not numerous. There are deer and wild turkeys; yet, when the district was first settled, the buffalo was so numerous, that it was nothing uncommon for three or four men to kill from ten to twenty per day. A rifleman could kill his four or five deer in the same time; and of bears, the ordinary hunter laid up several hundred pounds of bear bacon every winter. The waters abounded with beavers, otters and muskrats: and the forests teemed with wolves, panthers and wild-cats. It was a famous stock country, from its profusion of canes and native grasses.

Of birds, there are, the pigeon, duck, partridge, woodcock, dove, robin, blackbird; the eagle, owl, hawk, kingfisher, crow; the mocking-bird, thrush, humming-bird, snow-bird, whippoorwill, &c.

The population of Laurens, by the census of 1840, is 21,584; of these, 12,673 are free, and 8,911 slaves. This return shows a small increase in ten years. The district is entitled to one senator and four representatives in the state legislature.

Laurensville is the seat of justice for the district. It is a small but pleasantly situated place, at the head of Little river. seventy-five miles from Columbia, and one hundred and ninety-five from Charleston. Its population is small —about 300. It has a neat Court House, a public Library, a Meeting-House, School, Jail, and about forty dwelling houses. There are several small villages in the district, Belfast, Huntsville, &c., of little importance. Education improves, and a taste for letters is increasing among the people. The free schools are numerous, and a large number of pupils are educated at the expense of the state, which appropriates for this purpose, annually, about twelve hundred dollars. The Presbyterian is the most numerous religious sect, the Baptist next, and next the Methodist. Considerable zeal is manifested here in behalf of morals and education.

Laurens has given birth to several of the distinguished partisan warriors of the revolution. Among these were majors Downs and Hunter, who were in frequent fight with the tories and Indians.

LEXINGTON DISTRICT.

The first settlers of LEXINGTON were from Germany. The original district in which Lexington was comprised, was called Saxe-Gotha. The present name of the district was a tribute to the people of Lexington, in Massachusetts.

Lexington is situated mostly in what is called the middle country of South Carolina. It is bounded on the north-east by the rivers Congaree and Broad, which separate it from Richland and Fairfield; on the southwest by the North Edisto, which divides it from Orangeburg; on the south-east by Orangeburg; and on the northwest by Newberry and Edgefield. It averages thirty-four miles in length, thirty in breadth, and contains 652,800 acres. The country undulates generally, but slightly, and has a few superior advantages. The largest portion of the land is included in the sandy regions, and is covered with an immense growth of pines. The most valuable lands lie in the space between the Broad and Saluda rivers. On the banks of rivers and near the water courses, the lands are also fertile; but, in the lower parts, are liable to frequent overflow.

The chief products of the district are cotton and corn. Cotton and lumber are almost the only articles prepared for sale. Mill-seats are choice and numerous; timber of the best kind is in abundance, and great quantities of lumber are annually sawed for the Charleston and other markets. Among the products for home consumption are, wheat, rye and oats. The grape has been culitvated with success, and some tolerable wine has been prepared from it.

The district is well watered. The Congaree, Broad, Saluda and Edisto rivers, either border or pass through it. The first three are navigable for boats drawing two feet water; the Edisto, during high water, is passable for rafts. These rivers have all of them numerous tributary streams, which fertilize the neighboring lands, and furnish numerous admirable mill-seats. The creeks are, the Wateree, Priester, Camping, Bear, Holly, Congaree, Sandy Run, Cedar, Big Beaver, Black, Thorn, Twelve Mile, &c. The shoals of the Saluda are avoided by two canals, with locks, which give passage to freight boats.

Of fish there are, the shad, sturgeon, trout, bream, redhorse, mud, cat, and a variety of perch.

Granite is found in adundance along the Broad and Saluda rivers. One species, of a beautiful chocolate color, is considered rare and remarkable. Quarries of freestone lie on and near the banks of Congaree creek; some of it very white, and at a little distance resembling marble. It is easily worked, when first taken from the quarry, and hardens on exposure to the air. It is much used for building, and in quantity it is inexhaustible. There is no limestone; but a species of chalk, or potter's clay, is found, some of which, sent to Europe, was made into a set of china, and the clay pronounced by the manufacturer to be far superior to any found in England. A beautiful, variegated pink-colored stone, of a soft and soapy nature, is found at Congaree bluff. On the Wateree creek, there is slatestone. Iron, small in quantity and poor in quality, has been found, and there is a tradition, that lead ore was once procured abundantly at Ruff's mountain, near the line of Lexington and Newberry. This mountain is a conspicuous elevation, of great beauty, three hundred feet above the level of the surrounding country. It is one mile in length. On its top are, sienite, ferruginous sandstone, clay, slate and talc. From the abundance of the last, it has been called mount Talco. An excavation of considerable size, by unknown hands, seems to indicate the labors of former miners.

The forest trees of Lexington are very fine. Here the pine grows to great bulk and gigantic height. It is the most numerous tree; but there are besides, the poplar, walnut, maple, oak, (various species,) wild orange, evergreen, elm, hickory, ash, gum, &c. The fruits are, the peach, pear, plum, apple, quince, and cherry; grape, nuts, &c.

The game consists of the deer, turkey, wild pigeon, partridge, snipe, woodcock, dove and lark; the birds are, the eagle, owl, hawk, wren, lark, wood-pecker, sparrow, mocker, thrush, red-bird, jay, &c.

The population of Lexington, according to the census of 1840, is 12,011. Of these, 7,426 are free, and 4,685, slaves; showing an increase of more than 4000 persons in twenty years. Lexington is entitled, in the state legislature, to one senator and two representatives. Agriculture is the chief occupation of the people. The manufactures are chiefly domestic, and for home use. There have been some attempts at manufactures on a larger scale, but they have declined. The climate is mild and salubrious. The bilious, and other fevers, are chiefly confined to the water courses. Instances of longevity are frequent.

Lexington is the seat of justice. It stands near the centre of the district, in a high, healthy situation, thirteen miles from Columbia, and one hundred and twenty-two from Charleston. Its population is small, not exceeding 100 persons. It contains a Court House and Jail, and fifteen or twenty dwellings.

Granby, at the head of navigation on the Congaree, now in ruins and nearly deserted, was, during the revolution, a place of considerable importance. It was frequently the scene of conflict, and several times underwent siege during that period.

Platt's Springs, nine miles south-west from Lexington, is a place of considerable summer resort. It is very healthy, and has fine water. The Platt Spring Academy, has long possessed an enviable reputation, and receives pupils from every portion of the state. Attached to it is an excellent library. Education and agriculture are both improving in Lexington. The annual state appropriation for free schools is six hundred dollars. The German

Lutheran is the most numerous sect in this district. Their churches are frequent. There are other denominations, the chief of which are Baptist and Methodist. The people are uniformly industrious, and property is very equally distributed among them.

MARION DISTRICT.

Marion was settled chiefly by Virginians, about the year 1750. Its name was conferred upon it in compliment to the famous partisan. It is one of the extreme eastern districts of the state; is bounded on the northeast by North Carolina; east by Horry; south by Georgetown and Williamsburg; north-west by Darlington and Marlborough. Its length is forty-one miles; breadth thirty. It contains 787,000 square acres.

The face of the district is uniformly level, intersected in all directions by the finest creeks and rivers. The swamp lands, which are of considerable extent, are very rich; the uplands sandy, bottomed on clay. Portions of the highlands are productive, but cultivation is necessary for the residue.

The rivers Pedee, (Great and Little,) are navigable for vessels of considerable burden. So is the Kaddipah, or Lynch's creek. Besides these, there are Jeffrie's creek, Ashpole, Buck, Sweet, Big, Smith and other swamps, and numerous smaller streams. The lakes are, Jordan and Snow. The latter, with the Great Pedee, forms two islands, Hunter and Gaston. Snow's island is locally famous, as the frequent retreat and place of encampment of general Marion. Ashpole swamp was scarcely less famous, as the place of tory refuge. In some of these swamps, there are lakes of considerable size, one of which is the Duck Pond, up the Great Pedee, and near the line of Darlington.

The shad and herring, when in season, are caught in great abundance in this district. The Pedee is the last river to the south in which the herring may be caught. The other fish are, trout, bream, perch, cat, &c.

Marion, lying within the alluvial region, has no stone but shell limestone. When burnt, it is a good substitute for shell or stone lime, either for building or agriculture.

The most numerous of the forest trees in this district, is the pine; next the cypress, the oak, hickory, &c. The fruits are, peach, apple, pear, plum, &c. The game are, deer, turkeys, ducks, geese and pigeons, besides the birds which are common to the country.

The population, by the census of 1840, is 13,932. Of these, 8,681 are free, and 5,251 slaves. The census of Marion shows an increase, in ten years, of 2,500 persons, though emigration to the west has been frequent. Entitled to one senator and two representatives in the state legislature.

The climate is mild and agreeeble. The diseases of the country are bilious and autumnal fevers, which are chiefly confined to the water courses. Remote from these, the settlements are considered healthy. The instances of longevity are frequent.

Marion, the district town, is a small place on the east side of Catfish creek, a tributary of the Great Pedee. It has a handsome Court House of brick, a Jail and an Academy. It is ninety-four miles from Columbia and one hundred and twenty-three from Charleston. It contains some thirty houses and about 100 inhabitants. Spring and Harlaersville, are two other small settlements.

Agriculture is the chief or only occupation of the people. The manufactures are purely domestic. The poor are few. Education is improving. There are numerous private schools, and a liberal appropriation of twelve hundred dollars by the state legislature, provides an adequate number of free scholars with tuition. The morals of the district are good. In religion, the Methodist is the most numerous sect. Next to them the Presbyterians.

Marion district abounds in scenes made memorable during the revolution by repeated conflicts. It was in this district that general Marion achieved some of his most remarkable successes over the tories and British.

MARLBOROUGH DISTRICT.

MARLBOROUGH was first settled by the frontier inhabitants of Virginia and Pennsylvania, flying from the Indians after Braddock's defeat. The population was slow of increase, until after the Indian treaty of 1755. In 1798, it was erected into an independant judicial district, with its present name, which is pronounced to have been given in honor of the famous duke of Marlborough.

Marlborough forms the extreme north-east corner of the state, and lies mostly within the alluvial region. It is bounded on the north and north-east by North Carolina; on the north-east by Marion; and on the south-west by the Great Pedee, which separates it from Darlington and Chesterfield. The average length of the district is twenty-seven miles; its breadth, eighteen. It contains 311,040 acres.

The face of the district is level. Only a small angle, (the north-west,) dips into the granite or primitive region. Much of the soil is rich and productive, particularly the highland swamp, which is rarely subject to freshets. The margins of streams and rivers, by which this district is intersected in every direction, afford numerous tracts of admirable soil. The uplands are covered with pine growth; the soil light and sandy, but with a good clay bottom. The river lands, cultivated to the very edge of the water, are generally from one to three miles in width. These lowlands extend along the whole length of Chesterfield and Darlington,—a distance, by water, of fully sixty miles.

The Great Pedee is the principal river of the district. It is navigable for steamboats to Cheraw bridge, one hundred and forty-four miles from Georgetown, and eight from the North Carolina line. It is a remarkably crooked stream, of slow current accordingly, and, in this respect, equally favoring agriculture and navigation. The Little Pedee, which is here called Gum swamp, passes through the south-east corner of the district. It has two or three branches. The streams next in importance are, Crooked Creek, Beaver Dam, Three Runs, Naked, Muddy, White, Phill's, Husband's, Hicks and Marks. Most of these creeks run through swamp lands, which may be reclaimed and made of great value. They all furnish excellent mill seats for sawing lumber, ginning cotton, &c.

Shad and sturgeon, in great quantities, are caught during the spring in the Pedee. There are, also, trout, perch, rock, bream, cat, and several other kinds of fish.

The timber trees of the river lands and swamps are various and fine, consisting of cypress, sycamore, cotton, oak, (several kinds,) gum, hickory, chestnut, poplar, bay, &c. The uplands bear the long leaf pine. The fruit trees are, the apple, peach, nectarine; (exotics;) the native fruits are, the crab-apple, plum, grape, haw, chestnut, chingapin, &c. The game are, the deer, turkey, woodcock, snipe, duck, pigeon, partridge, &c. The birds are, the mocking-bird, thrush, red and blue-bird, hawk, owl, whippoorwill, &c.

Granite rocks are found in the bed of the Pedee, and in the north-west angle of the district. Brown sandstone has also been discovered in the Pedee. Freestone and pyrites, or sulphate of iron, have been found in small quantities.

The climate of Marlborough is hot and moist. Along the swamps and rivers, bilious fevers prevail to a great degree. But the sand hill regions are salubrious, and form the usual places of resort during the sickly season.

The population of Marlborough, by the census of 1840, is 8,408. Of these, 4,290 are free, and 4,118 slaves. The population has rather diminished than increased within the last ten years. It is entitled, in the state legislature, to one senator and one representative.

Cotton is the chief market product of Marlborough. The market town is Cheraw. Corn, wheat, rye and oats, are raised only for domestic use. There are no manufactures unless for home purposes.

The seat of justice is Bennettsville. It is a small, neat settlement, on the east side of Crooked creek, about twelve miles from Cheraw, ninety from Columbia, and one hundred and fifty-eight from Charleston. It is a place of health, and is moderately prosperous. Its Court House is one of the finest in the state. The offices are fire proof. The Jail is also a strong, good looking fabric, rendered secure against fire. The population of Bennettsville is small.

Marlborough, formerly the district town, is near the Great Pedee. It has but few inhabitants, and has been abandoned as the seat of justice, as its climate was sickly, and its position not sufficiently central.

Until very lately, the education of the young was not sufficiently regarded in Marlborough. The more wealthy parents sent their children to school in neighboring districts. Latterly, this matter has been much amended. The private schools are now good and increasing, and the free schools receive an annual appropriation of five or six hundred dollars from the state. The Methodist is the most numerous religious sect; the Baptist and Presbyterian next. Agriculture is improving, and the establishment lately of a new Agricultural Society in this district, corresponds happily with the general movement on this subject throughout the state.

Among the distinguished men furnished by this district during the revolution, are general Thomas and captain Irby; both very brave and successful partisan leaders.

Marlborough once had a colony of Welch, on a fine tract of land near the Pedee. Their descendants are now incorporated among the great body of the people. One of the leaders was a reputed descendant of the famous Owen Glendower.

Among those beautiful flower plains of the forest, called savannahs, which are numerous in Marlborough district, is one near the centre of the district, the great loveliness of which is expressed by the name. It is happily called "Beauty Spot." It is about four miles in circuit, and always green in tracts of grass and cypress.

NEWBERRY DISTRICT.

NEWBERRY began to be settled at first by Pennsylvanians, about the year 1750. Different tracts of it were subsequently taken by Scotch, German and Quaker settlers. Adventurers from this district explored the Tennessee in canoes, passed the Muscle Shoals, and proceeded as far as the French or Indian settlements at Natchez, Mississippi, several years before the revolution.

Newberry lies within the granite region. It is bounded on the south-west by the Saluda river, which separates it from Edgefield; on the north and east by the Enoree, by which it is separated from Union; on the east by Broad river, which divides it from Fairfield; on the south-east by the district of Lexington; on the north-west by Laurens. The average extent of Newberry is about twenty-four square miles. It contains 368,640 square acres.

The face of the country is elevated and undulating. It contains considerable quantities of granite, freestone and soapstone. Beds of iron ore have been found, and a variety of silicious stones, vitreous and mineral substances. Limestone is supposed to exist, but none has yet been found. This conjecture has grown out of the fact, that wells of water have been discovered, strongly impregnated with calcareous matter. A ponderous mineral substance, resembling gold, has been found, which, when in fusion, emits a smell like that of arsenic. Other mineral substances are met with of various appearances, resembling antimony, loadstone, &c. Plumbago and stone coal, in small quantities, have been discovered. There are two mineral springs in the district, which appear to be strongly impregnated with salts, sulphur, and vitriol of iron. They act as cathartics,—sometimes vomit, will cure sore eyes, cutaneous eruptions, and have been used with success in chills and colds.

The soil of this district is divided into four classes; clay, sandy, gravelly and stony. There is very little loam. The clay is called mulatto land; it is preferred for wheat and tobacco, and, except in very hot weather, for almost every vegetable production. The sand and gravel lands are adapted to corn, cotton, oats, rye and barley. These are the chief products.

The Saluda is navigable along the whole south-west line of this district, for boats carrying fifty bales cotton. The Broad, or Eswawpuddenah, on the opposite, is navigable in like manner for boats of a similar size. The next rivers in importance are, the Tyger and Enoree. These are only partially navigable. Both of these rivers may be made as much so as the two former. Bush and Little rivers are two beautiful streams. Besides these, there are numerous other water courses, the principal of which are, Duncan's, Cannon's and Indian creeks; Beaver Dam, Mudlick, Carron's, Sandy Run, Buffalo, Camping, Palmetto, &c. Bush, Little river, and Duncan's creek, are ninety feet wide. The fish are, sturgeon, pike, suck, trout, carp, perch, red-horse, eel, gar, horny-head, &c.

Newberry has all varieties of the oak, among which is one less common—a species of swamp oak, growing in ponds and wet places, called the 'overcap.' The other native forest trees are, the ash, walnut, (black and white,) birch, elm, linden, gum, (black, sweet and poplar,) sugar-tree, cherry, maple, dogwood, box, elder, alder, witch-hazel, spicewood, sassafras, hickory, (four kinds,) pawpaw, cedar, cotton wood, &c. Other trees, not native, are, pride of India, Lombardy poplar, balm of Gilead, &c. The fruits are, the apple, peach, quince, plum, cherry, damson and fig. The wild fruits are, the crab-apple, chingapin, persimmon, haw, plum, muscadine, grape, &c. The sweet-bay, or cinnamon tree; ginseng, gentian, buckeye, rare in Carolina; are to be found in Newberry.

The game consists of deer, turkies, foxes, raccoons, opossums, squirrels, &c. The birds that migrate are, the marten, swallow, wild duck, robin, thrush, mockingbird, humming-bird, snipe, nightingale, whippoorwill, plover, kingfisher, &c. Those that remain are, the turkey, partridge, dove, king, red-bird, sparrow, crow, hawk, owl, woodcock and black-bird. Wild pigeons are occasionly seen. The bald eagle was once a resident of the district, and very destructive to young pigs and lambs; but he is no longer to be seen.

The population of Newberry, by the census of 1840, is 18,350. Of these, 8,446 are free, and 9,904 slaves. This shows an increase in ten years of about one thousand persons. The district is entitled to one senator and four representatives in the state legislature.

Agriculture is the chief employment of the people. The market town is Columbia. The manufactures are purely domestic, but these flourish in almost every family, and include almost every commodity of use, wear, and service, which can by any possibility be made at home.

The climate of Newberry is temperate and healthy. Neither the cold nor hot weather is of long duration. A great many instances of longevity are recorded. Diseases are few and not hard of management. The habits of the people are industrious and moral. Education has received a due share of the public attention. The state appropriation to the free schools, is about twelve hundred dollars per annum.

The Methodist is the most numerous religious sect; next, the Presbyterian and Baptist. The Lutherans have, within a few years, established in Newberry a theological seminary. There are numerous valuable private schools besides.

Newberry is the district town, or seat of justice. It is pleasantly situated, on elevated ground, about three miles east of Bush river. It commands a fine view of the surrounding country. A spring of excellent water issues near it, and the health and beauty of the situation render it a pleasant and attractive residence. Its population is small, not exceeding 300. They are represented as a frank, hardy and hospitable people. The Court House and Jail are substantial, and the former is a handsome building. So are some of the dwelling houses also. There are two academies and a library society in the village. Newberry is forty-four miles from Columbia and one hundred and sixty-four from Charleston.

Newberry has produced several men of superior worth and endowments, who have done the state some service. Among these were the Caldwells. Colonel Philemon Waters served in Braddock's war, and was in the battles of Stono and Eutaw. He was an active and able partisan. James Marion served in Grant's war against the Cherokees.

Among the curiosities shown in this district is the "devil's moccasin,"—the print of a man's foot in the solid granite, which is shown near Pennington's old frontier fort, on the Enoree river.

ORANGEBURG DISTRICT.

ORANGEBURG received its first white settlers in 1704; but it was without any considerable body of inhabitants until 1735, when it was occupied by a large colony of Germans, who, originally subjects of the prince of Orange, conferred his name upon the district.

Orangeburg lies entirely within the alluvial region. It is of very irregular figure. It is bounded on the east by the Congaree and Santee rivers, which separate it from the districts of Richland and Sumter; on the south-east by Charleston and Colleton; on the south-west by the South Edisto river, which divides it from Barnwell; on the north-west by Edgefield; and on the north-east and north by Lexington. From south-east to north-west, it extends seventy-five miles. A part of this extent it is scarcely twelve miles wide. Its greatest breadth, from south-west to north-east, is forty miles.

This district, extending in length so far, embraces a great variety of soil and surface. The face of the country is level in the southern and western portions, hilly and broken in the eastern and northern. Along the margins of streams and swamps, it is equally fertile and unhealthy. In the more elevated regions, where it is sterile and sandy, it is very healthy. The climate throughout is mild and agreeable, and is commended to patients suffering from pulmonary causes.

There is no appearance of granite in this district. Considerable bodies of compact shell-limestone are found, in working some of which numerous petrifactions were discovered, and such shells and marine productions as are common to the sea shore. Freestone, grey and white, is to be found in several places, specimens of which have been used in public works. Potter's earth, or soapstone, and ironstone, (tolerably rich in ore,) are also afforded by this district. Gold has been worked for, and it is thought that a considerable portion of that precious metal has rewarded the industry that sought for it. Several reasons have been given for the suspension of a labor which promised so fruitfully.

The larger proportion of the soils of this district consist of pine lands, which are generally thin, light and sandy, but bottomed on clay. The lands of best quality are the high pine lands. The swamps most remote from the river are the most valuable. In its immediate neighborhood, though rich, they are endangered by freshets.

The lands bordering on the Congaree and Santee present very different aspects. The soil is stiff, clayey and very productive. In one place it displays the appearance of the primitive region; is free from swamp, the waters are clear, the country rises into hills, and bold bluffs overbrow the river.

The navigable waters of this district are extensive and valuable. The Santee and Congaree are navigated by steamboats which carry one thousand bales cotton. The two Edistos, for a portion of this district, may be also used by this sort of vessels, though they are not. They are traversed by small boats and lumber rafts. The Cawcaw, a branch of the Edisto, is also navigable twelve miles above its mouth. Bull swamp might be made so. Four Hole and Dean swamp, are also branches of South Edisto. The former is something of a curiosity; consisting of four great pits, which successively swallow and discharge the waters of the swamp. Plunging into one, they boil upward from the next. The pits are about half a mile apart. In a dry season, fish are taken in them, with hook and line, at a depth of thirty feet. They are near the Orangeburg line. There are other water courses, —Limestone, Cedar, Snake, Cooper, Buckhead, Bugaboo, Little Beaver, &c. These waters abound in fish. There are, in season, shad and sturgeon, trout, bream, rock, pike, cat, perch, &c.

The forest trees are in great variety. They consist of the pine, oak, (all kinds,) beech, willow, hickory, ash, birch, walnut, cypress, bay, maple, tupelo and poplar.

The game are, deer and turkey, duck, snipe, pigeon, woodcock, partridge and dove. The birds are, the bald-eagle, hawk, crow, mocking-bird, thrush, blue-bird, jay, sparrow and wood-pecker.

The population of Orangeburg, by the census of 1840, is 18,519. Of these, 6,585 are free, and 11,834 are slaves. The district, divided into two parishes, Orange and St. Mathew, is entitled to two senators and three representatives in the state legislature.

Agriculture is the chief employment of the people. The manufactures are few, and confined wholly to domestics. The productions are, cotton, grain and lumber. Indigo was once produced in large quantity in this district. It has been superseded almost entirely by cotton. Grain and provisions are raised for home consumption. Cotton and lumber are the only commodities which are prepared for sale. Charleston is the market for the district.

Orangeburg is the seat of justice. It was settled first in 1735. It is distant from Charleston, by the railroad, eighty miles; from Columbia, fifty miles. It is now a healthy and handsome village, having about 350 inhabitants. It is well laid out in regular squares, has a handsome Court House, Jail, and several tasteful private habitations. The old Jail was built in 1770, was converted into a fortified post by the British, and besieged and taken by Sumter, toward the close of the revolution. Here lord Rawdon had his quarters when pursued by Greene. The village has gone through many interesting vicissitudes; and, lying in the great line of thoroughfare, between the sea board and interior, was necessarily the scene of many curious events and severe conflicts. A free bridge crosses the Edisto near Orangeburg, and conducts, among other places, to the Poplar springs, which is a salubrious place of summer retreat for the neighborhood. It is five miles west of the Court House.

Totness, another village much frequented in summer, lies on the north side of High Hill creek, about three miles from the Congaree. It is a lofty elevation, some two hundred feet or more above the level of the river. The early settlers gathered gold in the neighborhood of Totness, but the ore seems to have eluded the search of the moderns.

Murrayville, Lewisville and Gadsden, are small places along the line of rail road, which traverses this district from Branchville to Fort Motte. These places are rather the seeds of future, than already existing villages.

Fort Motte, also near the line of rail road, stands on the northern boundary of the district. It was famous in the revolution, for the stout defence which, manned by a British garrison, it offered to the army of Marion. The patriotic devotion of Mrs. Motte, the owner of the property, by whose means it was destroyed and the garrison overcome, has been already recorded in song and story, and presented on the canvass of the artist.

Education and morals are improving in Orangeburg district. Agriculture has received a recent favorable impulse. There is an increasing taste for letters. Many of the planters are highly educated men. The state appropriates twelve hundred dollars per annum to the free schools of the district. The Methodist is the most numerous religious sect; next the Baptists and Lutherans. There is a congregation or more of Episcopalians.

Among the eminent men whom Orangeburg has given to the state, one of the most distinguished was colonel William Thompson, who, next to Moultrie, was most conspicuous in baffling the British in the battle of Sullivan's island in 1776. His residence was at Belleville, on the Congaree, opposite Fort Motte.

PENDLETON DISTRICT.

PICKENS AND ANDERSON.

The settlement of PENDLETON was slow from 1750 to 1763. From that period colonization went on vigorously. The Cherokee war, which terminated in the cession of all their lands east of the Unacaya mountains, and the close of the revolutionary struggle, had the farther effect of increasing the population of Pendleton. Prior to these events, the settlers had chiefly been drawn from the frontiers of Virginia, Pennsylvania and Maryland. Uutil 1798, this district was merged in that of "Ninety-Six." It was then erected into an independent judicial district, and received its name in compliment to Judge Pendleton.

Pendleton constitutes the extreme north-west boundary of South Carolina, and is the most mountainous district of the state. It is bounded on the south-west by the rivers Savannah and Tugaloo, which separate it from the state of Georgia; on the north-west by the Chatuga, which also divides it from Georgia; on the north by North Carolina; on the north-east by the Saluda river, which separates it from Greenville; and south-east by Abbeville district. The average length of Pendleton is fifty-one miles; breadth thirty-six. It contains about 1,175,040 square acres; being, in point of size, the third district of the state.

The face of the country is rolling and agreeably diversified, or mountainous and highly picturesque. The soil is various, bottomed mostly on red clay, and susceptible of great use in cultivation. Along the rivers there are large bodies of rich bottom lands, with interval tracts of pine. The mountain region is the north and west. The south and east are hilly, with gentle slopes, and long vallies and fertile plains. The soil is adapted to the culture of wheat, corn, cotton, barley, oats, hemp, indigo, gentian, ginseng, potatoes, &c. The climate is equal to any in the world; cold a short period, but stimulating; but for the greater part of the year, delightful equally for the traveler and laborer.

The rivers are, the Tugaloo and Seneca, (both branches of the Savannah,) the Saluda, Keowee and Chatuga. There are several smaller streams, viz: the Jocassee, the Toxaway, Chatuga, Chauga, Oconee, Estatoe, Rocky, Oolenoe, and numerous creeks, under the various names of Big and Little Generositee, Little river, Cane, White Water, Hurricane, Wilson, George's, Brush's, Broad Mouth, and Six, Twelve, Eighteen, Twenty-three and Twenty-six mile creeks. The district is excellently watered. The fish are, shad, cat, perch, suck-fish, &c.

The timber trees of the uplands are, oak, (post, red, black and Spanish,) hickory, blackjack, pine and chestnut. On the creeks and rivers are found, the oak, (white and water,) poplar, maple, gum, walnut, (black and white,) cherry, persimmon, beech, &c. The fruits are, the apple, peach, pear, plum, cherry, quince, and some varieties of grape. The birds and game are such as are to be found in the upper districts, and are numerous. The woodpecker migrates north in September and re-appears in spring.

The mountains of Pendleton are numerous and stupendous. Rocks of granite and gneiss abound. Beds of primitive limestone are discovered. The minerals are, iron, yellow ochre, pyrites, plumbago, kaolin, talc, asbestos, quartz, crystals, &c. The mountains yield a thousand objects of the picturesque for the delight of the curious: mountains of various shapes, bulk and height; streams of tumbling water; glens, and vallies, and walls, calculated to please and amaze the spectator. The Table rock is said to be one of the greatest curiosities of its class in the world. It rears an almost perpendicular wall of solid granite, upwards of a thousand feet from the plain. Its sides are fluted by the constant attrition of descending waters, which glow in the sunbeams like a belt of brilliants. Three sides of this mountain are inaccessible, and five cascades may be seen, at the same moment, struggling over the rocks at its feet. The sides of these streams are completely enclosed by a verdant hedge of branch and foliage. The ascent to the top is a difficult labor. Its summit is clothed with a delightful shade of trees and shrubbery. The flat surface on its top is about a mile square. The Giant's Stool is the name of a smaller rock, which stands in proper relation to his Table. A cedar-tree, at the extremity of the mountain elevation, is the usual limit of the explorer's progress. From this point the view is immeasurably grand and beautiful. You stand upon a precipice abruptly down, of one thousand one hundred feet. The eye takes in a vast extent of country—mountains and vallies, cultivated spots, and serpentine vallies. The whole district of Greeneville is spread before the sight. On the north-west is Brown's and Glassy mountain, the Six Mile mountain, and even the knob in Laurens district. To the east, in York district, King's mountain, famed for Ferguson's defeat, terminates the view. The Saluda mountains, Panther's Knob, Cæsar's Head, Dismal, Sassafras, Estatoe, and Oolenoe mountains appear in succession; and to the west, the Currahee mountains rise up, in Georgia, bounding the horizon.

The Sassafras Knob is the highest mountain in South Carolina, being three thousand two hundred feet above the ocean. The Estatoe river, which waters the beautiful valley of the same name, rises in its bosom. The Jocassee valley has been sung by native poets. It is celebrated for its romantic beauties, its rich vallies and sparkling waterfalls. There are two splendid cascades at the head of the Jocassee valley; that of Whitewater, and that of the main arm of Jocassee river, which, for elevation, exceeds that of Niagara. A stream called the "Devil's Fork," from the depth of its glens and the tangled gloom of its thickets, enters the valley and finds its way into the Jocassee river. The Toxaway is another lovely stream, full of similarly picturesque beauties. But the whole of this region is of a character to reward the traveler who looks for the beautiful in nature. The scenery of Switzerland does not surpass it in grace or grandeur.

The population of Pendleton, by the census of 1840, is 32,849. Of these, 24,451 are free, and 8,398 are slaves. Pendleton is entitled, in the state legislature, to one senator and seven representatives. For judicial purposes, the district has been divided into two parts, Pickens and Anderson. Pickens is in the north, and comprehends the mountainous parts of Pendleton. The population of Pickens is 14,356. Of these, 11,641 are free, and 2,755 slaves. Anderson contains a population of 18,493, of whom 12,810 are free, and 5,683 slaves. Anderson is the southern part of Pendleton, with an undulating surface, but not mountainous.

Pickens is the seat of justice for the judicial district of the same name. It lies on the west bank of the Keowee, a small but permanent settlement, with the usual complement of public offices. The dwellings are few. It is one hundred and forty miles from Columbia and two hundred and sixty from Charleston.

Anderson judicial district has a court town of the same name, which stands near the head waters of the Generositee creek. The buildings, beside the public offices, are few. The settlement is still small. The village is one hundred and fourteen miles from Columbia and two hundred and thirty-four from Charleston. There are several villages in both these sections; but they are of small size and population. In Pickens there are, Pulaski, Pumpkintown and Pickensville; in Anderson, Rock Mills, Centreville and Andersonville.

The length of Pickens is forty-two miles; breadth, twenty-five. It contains 660,000 acres. Anderson is twenty-nine miles long, twenty-seven broad, and contains 500,000 acres.

Pendleton, the ancient capital of the district, is pleasantly situated near the waters of Eighteen Mile creek, a branch of the Seneca. It contains a splendid Court

House building, a Jail, two houses of public worship, an Academy, a newspaper and printing office, a public Library and an Agricultural Society; several fine dwellings, and about three hundred inhabitants. The village is a particularly pleasant one, and is still a favorite place of resort. The scenery in its neigborhood is very interesting. A beautiful view of the mountains bounding the horizon to the north, is obtained from it; a glimpse of the valley of Jocassee, the Table mountain, and beyond it, the towering summits of Sassafras or mount Estatoe. Pendleton, as a summer residence, is doubly attractive from its salubrious climate and enlightened society.

Education in Pendleton has been gradually and constantly advancing. Her citizens are generally well informed; many of them highly so. Two thousand dollars are appropriated annually by the state to the support of the free schools of the district. The most numerous religious sects are, the Presbyterian, Methodist, Baptist and Episcopalian.

Agriculture is the chief occupation of the people. Charleston and Hamburg are the principal markets. There are some small manfacturing establishments. Wine has been made, of good quality. Rifles have been manufactured. Centreville was established as a manufacturing village; but the most important labors of this kind are purely for domestic purposes. A beautiful porcelain clay has been found on the Keowee.

Pendleton has given to the state some very distinguished men; among them, generals Pickens and Anderson. The former is the well known partisan warrior, famous equally in warfare with the British and Indians. General Anderson distinguished himself at Cowpens and other places. In this district also lived captain John Lynch, supposed to have originated the notorious frontier law which still bears his name.

This district has been the scene of frequent conflict. The Cherokee Indians were its occupants at the first coming of our ancestors. They were a numerous people. Their names are more generally and more properly preserved in this than in any other district of the state. The remains of their settlements are still frequently to be seen. Among these are, Keowee, old and new; Seneca, on the river of that name; Chaugee, on the Chauga creek; Oconee, Estatoe, Quacoratchie, Tugaloo, Noyauwee and Chickaree. The Jocassee, is the sweet Indian name for as sweet a region; besides these, there are names of rivers—the Toxaway, Cheochee, Isundiga, Oolenoe, Keshawee, Generositee, and many others.

The Cherokees were frequently in arms against the white settlers, and as frequently defeated. They received a terrible defeat from the Carolinians under colonel Grant, and another from general Pickens; for the particulars of which see History of South Carolina. Fort Prince George, famous for sanguinary events, stood in this district, on the left bank of the Keowee. Near the town of Etchoe, colonel Grant obtained his victory over the Cherokees in 1761.

RICHLAND DISTRICT.

The first settlements by whites, in RICHLAND District, were made about the year 1740. These were followed by German emigrants. Virginia subsequently furnished the chief settlers in the lower parts of the district, increasing the population largely, after peace was made with the Cherokees in 1755. The territory of Richland was once in the occupation of this nation of Indians. Its name is supposed to have been given it in compliment to its rich soils,—the highland swamps which border its rivers.

Richland is nearly equally divided between the primitive and alluvial regions. It lies in the very heart and centre of the state. It is bounded on the south by Orangeburg, from which it is separated by the Congaree; on the south and west by Lexington, from which it is separated by the Congaree and Broad; on the east by Sumter, from which it is divided by the Wateree; on the north by Fairfield; and on the north-east by Kershaw district. Richland averages thirty miles in length and twenty-one in breadth, and is computed to contain 403,200 acres.

The face of the country is broken, rising into ledges and hills, presenting an undulating and pleasing appearance. The soil is various; along the rivers, rich, deep and highly fertile. Scarcely inferior in quality are the bottom lands of creeks. Next to this are the high, flat, loamy, red lands, such as skirt the Broad river. The sand lands, which comprise the largest portion of the district, are inferior to these, but not unproductive. The low lands contiguous to the rivers are subject to inundation, which greatly lessens their intrinsic value. The products of Richland, like its soil, are numerous, consisting of cotton, corn, wheat, rye, oats, barley, potatoes, wine, &c. The climate is mild, and the region generally healthy. In the neighborhood of the rich bottom lands of creeks and rivers, the usual fevers prevail in autumn; the sand hill country, however, is as salubrious as any in the world; and with health, a fine atmosphere, and springs of the most cooling water, they attract numerous visitors from less favored sections.

Richland, bounded by three noble streams, the Congaree, Broad and Wateree, all navigable the whole extent of the district, has numerous advantages, as well of trade as agriculture. Steamboats ply to Columbia and Camden. Bay boats, batteaux and canal boats are employed beside. These three are the only navigable streams. A canal, three or four miles in extent, avoids the great falls of the Congaree, near Columbia, and overcomes the obstructions which nature had thrown in the way of its commerce. This canal has four locks, is parallel to the river, and passes between it and the town. By these locks, which are the largest in the state, boats of the largest class may ascend into the town. A dam is thrown across Broad river, at the upper edge of the town, and is connected with the canal by a guard lock. This dam serves also to join this last canal with that of the Saluda, by which the trade of both rivers becomes concentrated at the seat of government. The approach to the town of Columbia across the Congaree, is effected by a massive bridge, the piers and abutments of which are of solid granite, in large blocks, raised twenty-eight feet above the bed of the river. The river is one thousand three hundred feet wide, its bed is a solid rock, and the carriage way to the bridge exceeds in length one thousand three hundred and fifty feet. The bridge is covered.

These rivers, the Congaree, Broad and Wateree, are the only navigable rivers. There are innumerable smaller streams, which irrigate its lands, furnish rich soils along their borders, and refresh its sand hills. The principal of these are, Little river, Upper river, Cedar, Cane, Carter's, Colonel's, Lower Cedar, Mills, Tom's, Gill's,

Rice, Spears, Kinsler, and several more still smaller. Above the falls of Columbia the Congaree is studded with beautiful islands, which furnish a pleasing picture. Large quantities of shad and sturgeon, when in season, are caught in the Congaree and Wateree. At all times there are trout, bream, perch, red-horse, suck, cat-fish, &c.

Granite is found in abundance along Broad river. Freestone has been discovered near the springs of Rice creek. Flint and quartz are most abundant. Slate and soapstone are found. Masses of ironstone, indicating the ore, are to be seen in various places. In calcareous matter the district is deficient.

The timber trees are, pine, oak, (several kinds,) hickory, elm, red bay, dogwood, elder, locust, persimmon, poplar, sassafras, &c. There are several species of native grape, and the grape has been cultivated in this district with much success. The fox, summer, winter and muscadine are natives. The fruits are, the fig, crab-apple, peach, apricot, nectarine, plum, damson, cherry, raspberry, strawberry, &c. Other plants and trees, naturalized in the district, are, the willow, pride of India, palma christi, Lombardy poplar, catalpa, ash, &c. The ornamental shrubs, native and naturalized, are also numerous. The game are, the deer, fox, rabbit, squirrel, wild goose, turkey, pigeon, woodcock, partridge, dove, robin, hawk, owl, crow, woodpecker, whippoorwill, &c. The singing birds are, the mocking-bird, red-bird, thrush, oriole, blue, cat-bird, &c.

The population of Richland district, by the census of 1840, is 16,397. Of these, 5,733 are free, and 10,664 slaves. This shows an increase in ten years of about 1700. The representation in the state legislature is one senator and four representatives. Agriculture is the chief employment of the people. Wine has been manufactured with success; so has paper for printing; and there is a very large manufactory for cotton goods in the neighborhood of Columbia, which is in successful operation The other manufactures are small and unimportant, and intended chiefly for domestic uses.

The principal town of Richland is Columbia, the capital of the state. Columbia lies in latitude 33° 57′ N. on the east bank of the Congaree, just below the confluence of the Broad and Saluda rivers. It is situated upon a plain two hundred feet above the bed of the river, in a situation equally commanding and beautiful. It is laid out in regular squares, divided by streets one hundred feet, and sometimes one hundred and fifty feet, in width. The town is two miles square. Columbia was incorporated in 1787. The legislature first met here in 1790. The population is near 4000.

Columbia is not merely the seat of government for South Carolina. It is also her favored seat of learning. Here stands the South Carolina College, a well endowed home of letters, which has sent forth from its walls several of the ablest intellects of which the whole country may boast. This institution was established by the legislature in 1801, and in 1804 went into operation. The buildings are extensive, well built, durable and undergoing expansion and increase. The state appropriates fourteen thousand dollars to the support of the institution, and makes a further appropriation of two thousand dollars annually for a college library, which now numbers several thousand volumes, of a rare and select description. The institution is amply furnished with all the necessary means and apparatus for carrying on with ease and certainty the processes of a scientific education. Three hundred thousand dollars have been appropriated to the erection of the necessary buildings, which are all of brick. The premises cover altogether about twenty-five acres of ground, and are enclosed by a lofty wall of brick. The faculty consists of a president, five professors and two tutors. The number of students, under the present flourishing auspices of the institution, is about one hundred and fifty.

The State House is an inferior building, of wood, humble in its architecture, and only tolerably commodious. A building on an improved plan, and made of the granite of which the neighborhood furnishes an abundance, would seem due to the uses of such a building, and the dignity of the state.

The Lunatic Asylum of the state is in Columbia. It is a spacious edifice, fire proof, and of imposing appearance. The number of patients which it contains, is sixty-five. Of these, thirteen are brought from other states.

The Theological Seminary of South Carolina and Georgia has been planted in Columbia. The public buildings are, a Court House, two Banks, a Town Hall, Mason's Hall, Jail, Market House, and numerous hotels. There are Baptist, Methodist, Presbyterian, Episcopalian and Catholic churches, most of which are neat architectural structures. There are several excellent academies in Columbia, and in no place in South Carlina is more regard paid to the primary interests of religion and education. An appropriation to the free schools, of twelve hundred dollars, is made annually by the state.

The town is supplied with good spring water by means of steam water works. There is a spacious Theatre, but the performances are unfrequent. Several societies, agricultural, literary and otherwise, denote the mental activity of the people, and promise the richest future results. The press issues three newspapers, one of which is devoted almost wholly to temperance and morals. The others are political.

Columbia enjoys a considerable trade with the neighboring country and with Charleston. The *terminus* of the Great Rail Road, which was projected to run from Charleston to Louisville, in Kentucky, it is evidently destined to a farther increase of commercial prosperity.

The watering places or summer retreats of Richland, are usually called villages. Of these, the Rice Creek Springs may be mentioned as a place of much resort. It is fifteen miles north-east from Columbia. It has an excellent school and public house. The air is dry and bracing and remarkably cool.

Lightwood Knot Spring is a similar settlement. It is situated on a branch of Jackson's creek, six miles from Columbia. Minersville, twelve miles from Columbia, has long been the seat of an Academy, and is equally healthy with the former place. The sand ridges are generally summer retreats; cool and shady, having the most excellent water, and invariably secure from those diseases which prey upon the richer settlement.

Richland has produced her full complement of eminent men. Among these may be enumerated, the Dessaussures, Hamptons, Taylors; all of them distinguished as worthies of the revolution. Several of her sons acquired high reputation for conduct and bravery in numerous actions during the same period. The events which have taken place within her borders may be found in the History of the State.

Faust's Ford is famous in tradition, as being the old Indian track for the Catawba, across the Eswawpuddenah or Broad river. It was the secure route during the revolution for the tory or plunderer needing concealment. Below this ford is an extensive range of lofty hills which approach the river, on the brow of one of which the buffalo lick is still visible. The spot was evidently a great range for this forest cattle. Indian antiquities, mounds, or tumuli, are found in many places. Cook's Mount is a considerable eminence near the Wateree river.

SPARTANBURG DISTRICT.

SPARTANBURG first began to be settled about 1750; but its population did not much increase until 1770. The first settlers were a race of hardy hunters from Virginia, Pennsylvania and North Carolina. It was originally a part of Ninety-Six district. It received the name of Spartanburg after the revolution.

This district lies in a high and healthy region, forming the extreme northern boundary of the state. The face of the country is undulating, agreeably diversified by hill and dale, mount and plain. The climate is temperate and salubrious.

Spartanburg is bounded on the north by North Carolina; on the north-east by York; on the east and south-east by Union; on the west by Greenville, and on the south-west by Laurens and Greenville. Its extent from north to south averages thirty-five miles; from east to west thirty miles. It comprises 672,000 square acres.

The soil is fertile, resting generally on a clay bottom. Some of it is gravelly, some stony, but easy of improvement and producing well. All kinds of grain are cultivated with success. The productions are, corn, cotton and tobacco.

The forest trees are, oak, (white, red and Spanish,) pine, poplar, chestnut, black walnut, curled maple and wild cherry; all of which, used for cabinet work, form good substitutes for mahogany. The fruit trees are, peach, quince, cherry, plum, &c. The birds are few. The crow is a native; there are several kinds of hawk and owl; the turtle dove, quail and sparrow. Pheasants occasionally, and wild pigeons in great abundance, are found in autumn and winter. The mocking-bird, whippoorwill, and red headed woodpecker, make their appearance regularly in the spring.

The rivers are, the Broad, or Eswawpuddenah, the Pacolet, Enoree, Tyger, or Amoyescheck, &c. The smaller streams are, the Cherokee, Serratee, Thicketty, Buck, Fairforest, Cane, James, and Ferguson's creeks. The Broad river, a little below the line of this district, has a good navigation opened to the ocean. The Pacolet has a boat navigation up to its eastern boundary. The Pacolet and Enoree are both fine rivers, and may be yet considerably improved for the purposes of trade. The Pacolet, in this district, divides into two arms, called North and South Pacolet, both having their source in the mountains. The Tyger river is divided into three chief branches, called the South, North and Middle Forks. Twenty miles above their junction, these streams are scarcely three miles apart, and the two principal, only one mile. Fairforest, Dutchman, Fergus, James, and Cane creeks are all branches of the Tyger; the Thicketty, Cherokee and Serratee creeks are feeders of the Eswawpuddenah. The vallies along these rivers afford excellent soil. The ridges are poor. Several beautiful cascades occur in these rivers. Those of the Pacolet are particularly so. The mountain shoals on the Enoree are also curious and beautiful. The waters, in a distance of only twenty-four chains, fling themselves over a precipice of seventy-six feet.

In the Pacolet there was, at one time, a great fishery, in which were caught, the shad, trout, red-horse, rock and cat-fish.

Spartanburg has a great many fine quarries of granite, gneiss, and a kind of freestone. The soapstone, of an excellent quality, is inexhaustible in quantity. Some of it has been used for the ornamental parts of public buildings; the caps of columns, for example, of the Greenville Court House. Limestone and marble are abundant, and one of the heads of Thicketty creek has its source in a fine chalybeate spring, near the quarries of the latter. The Limestone Spring near the Cherokee quarry, is a place of much resort.

Iron ore, in great abundance, is procured and worked in this district. The largest mass and richest mines are in Thicketty mountain. This is a majestic mound which overlooks the country. The Spartanburg iron works are now in considerable vogue. The ore is of superior quality, and manufactures, though confined to the coarse implements, are fully equal to any of foreign production. The works now are so improved as to permit the proprietors to contend with the foreign manufacturer, in the markets of Charleston and Columbia. Plumbago, or black lead, has been discovered on the Cherokee creek. Gold, in small quantities, has been found; as, also, tetanium, pyrites, feldspar, talc, &c. Near the Cowpens, is Clarke's Iron Factory, which supplies to the markets of the state considerable quantities of hollow ware.

The Sulphur Springs, which have a large local reputation for numerous virtues, are twelve miles south-east of Spartanburg Court House, and near the line of Union district. They are particularly recommended for cutaneous affections. The waters of Cedar Spring are also famous for their medicinal properties, particularly in rheumatism, ulcers, and even in fever and ague. This and the Pacolet Springs are places of summer resort. At the former village is an excellent Academy; at both of them may be found pleasant society and attractive scenery.

The population of Spartanburg, by the census of 1840, is 23,669. Of these, 17,982 are free, and 5,687 are slaves. This shows an increase in ten years of 2,500. The district is entitled in the state legislature to one senator and five representatives.

The chief employment is agriculture. Manufactures are not inconsiderable and are on the increase. Education is rapidly improving. The habits of the people are simple, hardy and virtuous, and religion is regarded with proper veneration. The Baptist is the most numerous sect; but there are large numbers of Methodists and Presbyterians. An annual appropriation of fifteen hundred dollars is made by the legislature to the free schools of the district. Good schools are frequent and well attended.

Spartanburg village is the district town, or seat of justice. It is a pleasant village, agreeably situated, healthy and flourishing. Its population is about 1000. It is distant from Columbia one hundred, and from Charleston two hundred and twenty miles. It has the usual public buildings, Court House, Jail, &c.

There are some other small villages, such as Earlesville, and Poolesville. At the latter is a Manual Labor School, under the patronage of the South Carolina Presbytery.

Spartanburg furnished several very distinguished officers in the revolution, and more than one famous battle field attests the hardy valor of her people and the toils through which they have gone. The Cowpens, which is situate about four miles south of the North Carolina line, is a name famous in our history for one of the severest defeats ever given to a British army. Another affair highly honorable to the Americans, took place at Greene's Spring, in this district, where colonel Clarke of Georgia defeated, with great slaughter, a superior force of the British under colonel Dunlap. In this affair, the Americans were put in preparation for the enemy, who expected to surprise them, by the generous courage of Mrs. Dillard, a dame of Spartanburg, who rode a young horse, without saddle or bridle, at night, to apprise them of the coming danger.

SUMTER DISTRICT.

Sumter was first permanently settled about the year 1750, chiefly by Virginians. The district was named in honor of general Thomas Sumter, of famous memory.

Sumter lies within the alluvial region. It is bounded on the north-east by Lynch's creek, which divides it from Darlington; on the south-east by Williamsburg; on the south-west by the Santee and Wateree rivers, which separate it from Charleston, Orangeburg and Richland; and on the north-west by the district of Kershaw. Sumter is a very large district, forty-four miles long, thirty-eight broad, and containing, by computation, 1,070,080 square acres.

The face of the country, from the east to the centre, is level; thence, towards the north-west, it rises into hills, some of which are lofty and picturesque; all of which are salubrious. The soil is generally productive, and well adapted to the cultivation of cotton, which is the sole staple of the district. It is either a rich black loam, or a reddish clay, which is productive also. The tracts of sand are sterile and extensive. The productions are, cotton, corn, peas, potatoes, wheat, oats, rye, millet, &c.

The forest trees are, the pine, cypress, sycamore, oak, (black and white,) hickory, poplar, magnolia, gum, beech, cotton-tree, and a variety of others. Many of these trees, the oak, sycamore and cypress, grow to an enormous size. The beautiful gardenia is a native of this district. The fruits are, peach, plum, apple, pear, fig, nectarine, &c. Grapes and berries, of all kinds, are abundant.

The game consists of the deer, turkey, duck, dove, partridge, snipe, woodcock, &c. The singing birds are numerous, and such as inhabit the similar region of country throughout the state. There is also the usual supply of hawks, owls, crows, and woodpeckers; and the wildcat, fox, opossum, rabbit and squirrel are equally numerous.

The Wateree and Santee rivers are navigable, for boats of considerable burthen, the whole length of the district. The Kaddipah (Lynch's creek) is also traversed, but by boats of smaller size. The Wynee, or Black river, may be made so. Sumter is well watered beside by numerous other streams, the lands in the neighborhood of which are exceedingly fertile. Such are the Pocotaligo, Rafting, Tawcaw, Hungary, Cowpen, Douglas, Savana, Hope, Half Way, and Tear Coat.

The Lakes are, Brevington's, (a curious expanse of water,) Scott's, on the Santee, the "Raft," Wood Lake, Big Bay, Green Savannah, Mill Bay, and Pine Bluff. These are all, with the exception of the last, considerable bodies of water, varying in length from one to four miles. Black Oak island, bounded by Santee and Little rivers, is the south-east corner of the district.

These rivers and streams are all well provided with fish. Shad and sturgeon ascend them in the spring. The other fish are, trout, rock, bream, perch, red-horse, suck, mud and many others.

Sandstone is found near the Wateree, and among the Santee Hills. The latter is of a soft and crumbling nature; the former is hard, heavy and mixed with iron. It is sometimes found mixed with small shells and fuller's earth, and is used for building. At Bloom Hill there is a quarry of burrstone; and in the lower part of the district some compact shell limestone. There are several mineral springs. Of these, the most noted is Bradford's. The waters are chalybeate, with a little sulphur, and, drank freely, prove highly tonic. A remarkable range of hills, called the High Hills of Santee, are found in this district. They extend to the Kershaw line, a distance of twenty-two miles, vary in width, being, in the widest parts, about five miles. These hills are healthy places of retreat. The soil may be rendered tolerably productive by pains-taking cultivation.

Sumter district is subdivided into four counties, viz: Clermont, Clarendon, Upper and Lower Salem. It contains, by the census of 1840, a population of 27,892. Of these, 9,017 are free, and 18,875 slaves. This shows a slight decrease in ten years. Sumter is entitled to two senators and five representatives in the state legislature.

Agriculture is the chief business of the people. The manufactures are almost wholly domestic. Education is good and improving. The appropriation of the state, to the free schools, is about two thousand dollars. The Methodist is the most numerous religious denomination; but there are respectable bodies of most other sects. A due regard is every where paid to religion and morals. Sumter has more than an usual share of the taste for arts and literature. Some of her more wealthy planters appropriate large sums to these objects. Collections of pictures are forming, and the private libraries are frequent and select.

Sumterville is the seat of justice. It is near one of the head waters of the Wynee, which might be made navigable to within a short distance of the Court House. Sumterville is forty-five miles from Columbia and one hundred from Charleston. It has a handsome Court House and Jail, two Churches, an Academy, a public Library, and issues a weekly newspaper. The population is small. It was founded in 1800.

Statesburg, a village of the Hills, beautifully situated among them, is four miles east of the Wateree. It is a small and unimproving hamlet, founded in 1783, by general Sumter. It contains three Churches, (one Episcopalian and two Baptist,) an Academy, a Library and an Agricultural Society. The population, like that of Sumterville, is also very small—a fact not easily accounted for, since it stands in a situation of great salubrity, much beauty, and in the centre of a wealthy and refined community.

Bishopville, near the Kaddipah, (Lynch's creek) is a very healthy and pleasant hamlet. It is twenty-four miles north of Sumterville, is flourishing, does a small but lively business, and contains near two hundred inhabitants. It has its Church and Academy, and within two miles are two other Churches and several schools.

Manchester is a decayed town which has not realized the expectations of its founders. It is nine miles south of Statesburg, and thirteen south-west from Sumterville.

On the north bank of the Santee, stands Fort Watson, a strong British post in the revolution, besieged and captured by Marion in 1781. (See History.) It is raised on an ancient tumulus fifty feet high. Tawcaw, Nelson's Ferry and other places were the scenes of spirited actions between the Americans and British during this war.

Sumter has produced several eminent men, among whom, most conspicuous, was the celebrated general from whom the district takes its name. Other names may be referred to with pride by the people of this district. The Richardsons and Mannings have nobly served the country in various periods, as well of war as peace.

UNION DISTRICT.

This district was first settled in 1755, by emigrants from Virginia. The treaty of governor Glenn with the Cherokee Indians, contributed greatly to increase the population. It lies within the granite region of the state; is bounded on the north-east by Broad river, by which it is separated from the districts of Chester, York and Fairfield; on the north-west by Spartanburg; on the south-west by the Enoree, which separates it from Laurens; and on the south-east by Newberry. The average length of the district is thirty miles; breadth eighteen. It contains 345,000 acres.

The face of the country is hilly; in the north, mountainous. Clay, mixed either with rock, gravel or sand, is prevalent. On the rivers are considerable bodies of low and fertile lands, chiefly of rich clay. The ridges which separate water courses are generally of a thin, gravelly and sometimes stony soil. The lower parts of the district are adapted to the culture of cotton and Indian corn; the highlands, to wheat, rye, oats, barley, peas, pumpkins and potatoes. The finest granite is found in this district, particularly adapted to building purposes. Iron, lead ore, asbestos, talc, the sulphate of iron, quartz and gneiss have also been discovered.

The forest trees are, the oak, (various species) hickory, poplar, maple, black walnut, chestnut, sycamore, birch, dogwood, persimmon, locust, beech, ash, &c. In small number, the short leaved pine.

The fruits are, the peach, apple, plum, pear, nectarine, and the various nuts and berries. Wild grapes are abundant.

The game consists of the deer, turkey, fox, raccoon, opossum, squirrel, &c. The birds are, the eagle, hawk, kingfisher, marten, swallow, wild duck, robin, mocking-bird, thrush, cat-bird, woodpecker, jay, red-bird, sparrow and several others.

The Eswawpuddenah, or Broad river, traverses the longest line of this district, and is navigable for boats of considerable size to the Ninety-Nine islands. Lockhart's shoals, which were once an obstruction to this navigation, are now overcome by a canal with seven locks. The Pacolet, which crosses three fourths of the district, is now navigable to Grindall's shoals, a distance of twelve miles. It might be rendered further navigable, if these shoals were overcome. The Tyger and Enoree are considerable streams, which run parallel with each other twenty-six miles, the whole breadth of the district. In some places they are only three or four miles apart. A little succor from art would render both these streams navigable. The Tyger is already so for a distance of a few miles. Fairforest, a beautiful stream, is a branch of the Tyger, and from its proximity to the Court House, and the feasibility of a plan for connecting its waters with those of Broad river, it may be considered a very valuable stream. It furnishes many fine mill-seats. Gilky and Thicketty are two considerable streams, in the upper part of the district, which unite before entering Broad river. One of the branches of the Thicketty rises in a mountain of iron ore, and another in a marble and limestone quarry, both in the adjoining district of Spartanburg. There are several others of inferior importance, as Pategets, Tucker and Hacker—waters of the Tyger—Brown's, Farmer, People and Cherokee, Mill and Sandy, Sugar, Rocky, Buffalo, Beaver Dam and Harris—waters of the Fairforest—and Frenchman and Elisha, which are tributaries of the Enoree. The district is well watered.

The fish are, shad, (in season,) trout, rock, cat, red-horse, perch, pike, eel, carp, &c.

The climate is equable, mild, temperate and healthy. The fevers are confined to the water courses, and occur in autumn only.

By the census of 1840, the population of Union is 18,936. Of these, 10,582 are free; 8,354 slaves. The district is entitled to one senator and four representatives in the legislature of the state.

Unionville is the district town, or seat of justice. It is a small town in the centre of the district, in an elevated situation, at the head spring of Shoaly creek, a branch of the Fairforest, nine miles from Broad river, sixty from Columbia and one hundred and eighty from Charleston It contains a handsome Court House of stone, a Jail, about thirty houses and three hundred inhabitants. A Presbyterian Church and an Academy are among its public buildings. There is also a Library, and an Agricultural Society.

Pinckneyville, on Broad river, below the mouth of the Pacolet, is a pleasant village. Lockhart's canal, which overcomes the shoals of Broad river, is within four miles south of this settlement. The fall, which is obviated by this canal, (which is nearly three miles long,) is, in the space of two miles, fifty-one feet. Gowdeyville is the name of another small hamlet.

The chief employment of the people of Union is agriculture. The manufactures are excellent and various, but almost wholly for home consumption. The inhabitants are a healthy and improving people. The morals and education of the people have, in late years, undergone great alteration for the better. In religion, the Methodist is the most numerous sect, and after them the Presbyterian. The annual appropriaton of the state for the free schools of this district, is twelve hundred dollars.

This district was the scene of many spirited events in the revolution. Here, near Broad river, Sumter, in 1780, defeated a large force of tories. At Musgrave's mills, on the Enoree, in August of the same year, colonel Williams defeated another large body under the command of colonel Innis. In the ensuing November, at the Fish Dam Pond, Sumter defeated

Weyms and made him prisoner; and on the twentieth of the same month, obtained the famous victory, at Blackstocks, over colonel Tarleton. The Broad, Tyger, and Enoree were scenes of frequent conflict between the patriots and tories.

WILLIAMSBURG DISTRICT.

WILLIAMSBURG was settled in 1733, by that mixed people, called "the Scotch Irish;" but the people were properly Irish in character, for, with the exception of but one man, their descendants took up arms with the whigs of the revolution, and formed the nucleus of that famous corps, locally known as the brigade of Marion. The district was named in compliment to William III, of England.

Williamsburg lies wholly within the alluvial region. It is bounded on the south-west by the Santee, which separates it from Charleston; on the north-west by Sumter; on the north-east by Lynch's creek and the Great Pedee, which divide it from Marion; and on the south-east by the district of Georgetown. It is in length thirty-seven, breadth thirty miles, and contains about 710,000 acres.

The face of the country is level. The uplands are sandy, with a clay bottom. The swamp lands are of a rich quality. The climate is mild and agreeable, but along the water courses and swamps liable to autumnal fevers. The chief market production is cotton. Rice, corn, wheat and potatoes are also raised in considerable quantities. Cattle and hogs are sent in small number to the Charleston markets.

Marine productions are every where found, upon digging, in this district. A vein of shell limestone passes through it. Along the edge of Santee swamp, about nine miles from Gourdin's Ferry, are still to be seen several mounds, the work of unknown generations. The waste lands of this district are of great extent, valuable chiefly as ranges for cattle. But a small extent of swamp land is reclaimed, and that is partially liable to freshets.

The forest tree is chiefly the long leaf pine. Along the low lands or in the swamps, are found the cypress, ash, beech and tupelo. On the high lands near the swamps are oak and hickory. The fruits are, the peach, pear, apple, fig, strawberry, haw, melon and many others.

The game are, the deer, turkey, duck, goose, pigeon, &c. The birds are such as may be found in all the districts in the lower part of the state.

The rivers are, the Santee, Kaddipah, (Lynch's creek) Wynee or Black, Pedee and Black Mingo All of these are more or less navigable. The Santee, Kaddipah and Wynee are navigable their whole length in the district. The Black Mingo, once partially navigable, is now obstructed by refuse timber. The minor streams are numerous, and valuable, on many accounts, to their several neighborhoods.

All of these waters are well supplied with fish; trout, bream, perch, shad, and herring, when in season.

The population of Williamsburg, by the census of 1840, is 10,327. Of these, 3,359 are free, and 6,968 slaves. The district is entitled in the state legislature to one senator and two representatives. The population has increased 1000 in ten years.

Agriculture is the chief employment of the people. The manufactures are purely domestic. Of religionists, the Presbyterian is the most numerous sect, the Methodist next. The Baptist is respectable in numbers. The vices of the district are few. There are no distilleries, few drunkards, and gambling is discountenanced. There are numerous public and private schools. An appropriation of about five hundred dollars is annually made by the legislature to the free school fund of the district.

Kingstree is the district town and seat of justice for Williamsburg. It is situated on the left bank of Wynee river. It takes its name from a single tree, generally left upon a spot intended for public purposes, and called the king's tree, to designate its official character. The village occupies one of these spots, and the tree, (a white pine,) stood near the bridge and on the bank of the river.

The town is small, contains a few neat buildings, a handsome Court House of brick, a Library, Jail, &c. It is eighty miles south-east from Columbia, and seventy-six from Charleston.

New Market, (near Mount Hope Swamp,) and Indian Town are hamlets of small population. The remains of the Indian town of Old Mingo are still visible, within a mile of Indian Town Meeting House. To this village the waters of Black Mingo were once navigable.

Williamsburg has given birth to several highly distinguished men of the revolution; among whom may be mentioned the brave sergeant McDonald, who died at Fort Moultrie, with a sentiment of liberty on his lips, which alone has preserved his memory. The members of the James family were all able soldiers, and staunch patriots. Captain Willam McCottry, was a most daring partizan. It was in this district that Marion obtained his first recruits. Here, too, he effected some of his most surprising achievements. Snow's Island and Lake, in the eastern part of the district, was one of his choice retreats, to which he retired to recruit, or to elude the enemy, and from which he emerged only to destroy them.

YORK DISTRICT.

York was first settled in 1760, by emigrants from Pennsylvania and Virginia. Its name is supposed to have been derived from York in the former state, from whence some of the settlers came.

York is on the northern boundary line of the state, which separates it from North Carolina. The Catawba bounds it on the east, and divides it from Lancaster and North Carolina. Broad river bounds it on the west, and separates it from Spartanburg and Union; on the south it is bounded by the district of Chester. Its average length is thirty-three miles; breadth twenty-one. It contains 443,520 square acres.

The soil is mostly clay and well adapted to agricultural purposes. The face of the country is diversified, undulating, of mingled hill and dale, mountain and valley. Its rocks and stones are abundant, consisting of granite, compact limestone, marble, soapstone, and ironstone. The granite and iron ore are in sufficient quantities to supply any demand. There is a mountain, two miles in circuit, near Hill's old iron works, which is an entire mass of iron ore. Here colonel Hill cast cannon and shot for the patriots during the revolution. The district abounds in excellent clay for bricks, and lime is procured at King's Mountain.

The forest trees are, the various kinds of oak, hickory, poplar, chestnut, and some short leaf pine, &c. In certain spots the trees are of prodigious growth. One remarkable tree, a sycamore, which, at three feet from the earth, measures twenty-eight in circumference, stands in the north-east corner of the district, near the Little Catawba creek. It has three forks or prongs, each equal to a high tree. Many trees on the Catawba are also of immense size. One of them, a sugar-tree, which had been several times tapped for the juice, measured, in girth, ten feet, or three feet through.

The fruit trees include several kinds of apples, pears, peaches, cherries; besides chestnuts, shell bark hickory, walnuts, &c. The birds are, the partridge, dove, mocking-bird, crow, hawk and many others. Others appear at certain seasons, as the goose, duck, pigeon, whippoorwill, &c.

York is bounded by navigable streams on three sides. Broad is navigable for cotton boats up to the Ninety-Nine islands. The Catawba is navigable its whole course in the district. The other streams are, the Shugau, Crowder, Buffalo, Alison, Turkey, King and Camp, and several other creeks. All these streams abound in fish, such as shad, (in season,) trout, rock, red-horse, &c.

York is conspicuous as a region of great healthfulness. Its climate is particularly bland and temperate. The summer day is not oppressive, and the summer night is cool and refreshing. The winters are mild. The mountains protect the country from the cold winds of the north-west. Instances of great longevity are numerous.

The productions of the country are, cotton, wheat, corn, rye and tobacco. The only manufactures are domestic; but these are general and the manufactured commodities are good. The white clover and other native grasses are abundant in this district.

By the census of 1840, the population of York is 18,383. Of these, 11,558 are free, and 6,825 slaves. Entitled in the state legislature to one senator and four representatives.

The habits of the people of York are moral and industrious. The district is provided with good and improving schools. The state makes an annual appropriation of twelve hundred dollars to this purpose. The most numerous religious sect is the Presbyterian; next the Methodist; then the Baptist and Episcopalian.

Yorkville is the seat of justice. It stands centrally, on the dividing ridge between the waters of the Broad and Catawba, seventy-five miles from Columbia and one hundred and ninety-three from Charleston. Its situation is elevated, salubrious and in the midst of the finest scenery. It is well laid out in squares, and contains a population of six hundred. The Court House is an elegant structure of stone and brick. The Jail is a substantial building of brick. There are several places of worship, one newspaper office, Academies, Taverns, Post-office, and all the essentials of a very flourishing country town.

Until lately, the settlements of the Catawba Indians, in a narrow territory along the river of their own name, were objects of interest and curiosity. These Indians have long been the special care of the state, who has been, as far as possible, the nursing mother of their decaying fortunes. Recently they have resolved to unite the remnant of their tribe with another kindred remnant farther north, and in compliance with their desires, the state has treated with them for their lands. They were once a numerous and brave people, always faithful to the whites, and frequently arming in alliance with them. They were true to the state in the war of revolution, and suffered from all its disasters in the south. Their chief village was placed on the right bank of the Catawba, twenty-four miles from Yorkville. Their lands were good, but, with the indolent habits of their race, they preferred hiring them to others, instead of farming themselves. Their decay was inevitable and rapid. They were the great rivals of the Six Nations, who feared them and whose territories they frequently invaded.

King's Mountain is a well known name in the history of our revolution, famous for the bloody fight between the Americans and British when the latter were defated under colonel Ferguson. The battle ground is twelve miles north-west of Yorkville, and one hundred and ninety miles from Charleston. It is a long stony ridge, one mile in length and very narrow at the summit. The British occupied the whole extent of this ridge. The Americans advanced up the mountain in four bodies. Of the British four hundred were slain. The battle lasted the whole day. King's Mountain extends about sixteen miles from north to south, and its spurs spread laterally in many directions. Twelve miles of their extent is in North Carolina. The highest peak is estimated to be three thousand feet above the level of the ocean. Its summit is accessible to man only on one of its sides. King's Mountain abounds in marble and limestone. It gives birth to many streams. The highest peak of this mountain is called Crowder's Knob. From this elevated precipice bursts Crowder's Creek, which, after a course of eighteen miles, falls into the Catawba.

Henry's Knob is a singular and isolated eminence six miles east of King's Mountain, from the base of which issues a medicinal spring of many virtues.

Among the eminent men of York who did good service in the revolution, we find the names of Lacey, Hill, Bratton, Brannon and Hamright. Lacey was one of the leaders of the Americans at King's Mountain, and Bratton distinguished himself at Houck's defeat.

APPENDIX.

AGGREGATE POPULATION OF THE STATE.

DISTRICTS.	POP. IN 1830.	Census of 1840.			
		FREE.	SLAVES.	FEDERAL NUMBERS.	TOTAL.
Abbeville,	28,149	14,203	14,203	23,291	29,329
Barnwell,	19,236	10,968	10,503	17,267	21,471
Beaufort,	37,032	6,212	29,682	24,021	35,800
Charleston,	86,338	24,122	58,539	59,245	82,673
Chester,	17,182	10,025	7,772	14,658	17,747
Chesterfield,	8,472	5,703	2,871	7,425	8,574
Colleton,	27,256	6,302	19,246	17,850	25,548
Darlington,	13,728	7,262	7,560	11,798	14,822
Edgefield,	30,509	15,314	17,538	25,836	32,853
Fairfield,	21,546	7,660	12,505	15,163	20,165
Georgetown,	19,943	2,281	15,993	11,876	18,274
Greenville,	16,476	12,534	5,305	15,716	17,839
Horry,	5,245	4,181	1,574	5,125	5,755
Kershaw,	13,545	4,238	8,043	9,063	12,281
Lancaster,	10,361	5,672	4,235	8,213	9,907
Laurens,	20,863	12,673	8,911	18,019	21,584
Lexington,	9,065	7,426	4,685	10,237	12,011
Marion,	11,208	8,681	5,251	11,831	13,932
Marlborough,	8,582	4,290	4,118	6,760	8,408
Newberry,	17,441	8,446	9,904	14,389	18,350
Orangeburg,	18,453	6,585	11,934	13,745	18,519
Pickens,	14,473	11,641	2,955	13,414	14,356
Anderson,	17,169	12,810	5,683	16,219	18,493
Richland,	14,772	5,733	10,664	12,142	16,397
Spartanburg,	21,150	17,982	5,687	20,257	23,669
Sumter,	28,277	9,017	18,875	20,342	27,892
Union,	17,906	10,582	8,354	15,594	18,936
Williamsburg	9,018	3,359	6,968	7,539	10,327
York,	17,790	11,558	6,825	15,653	18,383
Total,	581,185	267,360	327,158	462,688	594,439

COMPARATIVE VIEW OF THE POPULATION FOR FIFTY YEARS.

1790.	1800.	1810.	1820.	1830.	1840.
249,073	345,591	415,115	502,741	581,185	594,439

DIFFERENT CLASSES OF INHABITANTS ACCORD-

DISTRICTS.	WHITES.		FREE COLORED.		SLAVES.	
	Males.	Females.	Males.	Females.	Males.	Females.
Abbeville,	6,971	6,909	149	174	7,434	7,714
Anderson,	6,308	6,439	38	25	2,783	2,900
Barnwell,	5,328	5,205	207	228	5,178	5,325
Beaufort,	2,817	2,833	230	232	14,180	15,502
Charleston,	10,926	9,995	1,343	1,858	27,445	31,094
Chester,	4,940	4,949	70	66	3,750	3,972
Chesterfield,	2,695	2,842	88	78	1,442	1,429
Colleton,	3,041	2,833	205	223	9,361	9,885
Darlington,	3,580	3,598	43	45	3,667	3,893
Edgefield,	7,617	7,403	155	139	8,728	8,806
Fairfield,	3,914	3,673	39	34	6,102	6,403
Georgetown,	1,042	1,051	86	102	7,580	8,413
Greenville,	6,138	6,353	23	20	2,587	2,718
Horry,	2,073	2,081	23	4	754	820
Kershaw,	2.010	1,978	127	123	3,899	4,144
Lancaster,	2,867	2,698	52	55	2,113	2,122
Laurens,	6,239	6,333	55	46	4,463	4,448
Lexington,	3,691	3,710	11	14	2,285	2,400
Marion,	4,269	4,324	43	45	2,567	2,684
Marlborough,	2,097	2,091	47	55	2,076	2,042
Newberry,	4,175	4,033	104	134	4,810	5,094
Orangeburgh,	3,255	3,066	136	128	5,929	6,005
Pickens,	5,721	5,827	51	42	1,328	1,387
Richland,	2,794	2,532	199	208	5,330	5,334
Spartanburg,	8,935	8,989	32	26	2,821	2,866
Sumter,	4,337	4,307	180	193	9,206	9,699
Union,	5,313	5,172	52	45	4,069	4,285
Williamsburg,	1,740	1,587	13	19	3,435	3,533
York.	5,663	5,786	58	51	3,382	3,443
Total,	130,496	128,588	3,864	4,412	158,678	168,360

SOUTH CAROLINA.

ING TO THE UNITED STATES CENSUS OF 1840.

Deaf, dumb, blind & insane white persons.				Deaf, dumb, blind & insane col'd persons.				Pensioners for revolut'y or mili'y serv's.	Scholars in acad'ies & grammar schools.	Scholars in primary or common schools.	Scholars at public charge.
Deaf & dumb.	Blind.	Insane and idiots.		Deaf & Dumb.	Blind.	Insane and idiots.					
		At public charge.	At private charge.			At private charge.	At public charge.				
7	16	4	16	4	15	9	1	11	412	1,115	153
7	7	1	10	3	2	7	0	31	233	687	124
1	8	1	13	6	12	8	2	4	95	440	41
1	0	0	1	0	2	0	0	1	172	377	126
4	12	20	5	10	20	9	2	25	1,008	904	654
8	11	5	16	4	5	10	0	13	70	527	134
2	1	0	2	0	0	2	0	5	—	—	—
0	0	0	3	2	7	5	0	1	112	365	277
6	4	7	12	5	6	9	0	7	149	305	65
8	6	3	10	4	3	5	3	28	65	152	79
0	0	0	0	0	0	0	0	2	25	98	30
0	1	0	0	0	3	1	0	0	165	73	100
8	6	4	28	3	6	7	0	18	148	509	75
4	3	0	2	1	1	1	1	0	—	101	20
3	0	0	2	3	0	0	0	6	127	304	139
4	1	2	1	1	3	4	0	11	6	446	128
15	10	2	16	5	10	6	2	16	206	905	95
4	0	0	8	0	0	2	0	2	105	146	43
2	4	3	11	3	6	4	1	4	71	238	17
3	3	3	9	0	1	5	0	5	104	229	33
5	1	0	9	2	1	2	0	3	134	757	240
3	3	0	10	2	9	1	0	5	40	236	39
7	2	0	22	0	1	1	1	22	51	579	114
2	7	32	28	0	6	5	0	1	161	366	126
10	3	1	5	0	1	0	2	31	179	375	32
0	3	0	5	3	24	5	0	13	145	693	186
9	8	2	25	4	4	5	0	24	240	738	263
8	3	1	7	9	7	6	0	2	70	161	28
9	10	0	9	4	1	2	1	26	33	679	163
140	133	91	285	78	156	121	16	318	4,326	12,520	3,524

AGGREGATE

VALUE AND PRODUCE, AND NUMBER OF PERSONS

EMPLOYED IN

AGRICULTURE, COMMERCE, MANUFACTURES, &c.

EXHIBITING A FULL VIEW OF THE

PURSUITS, INDUSTRY, AND RESOURCES

OF THE

STATE OF SOUTH CAROLINA,

AS COLLECTED UNDER THE ACT FOR TAKING
THE SIXTH CENSUS.

AGGREGATE OF THE STATISTICS OF THE STATE

DISTRICTS.	AGRICULTURE. LIVE STOCK.				
	Horses & Mules.	Neat Cattle.	Sheep.	Swine.	Poultry, all kinds, estimated value.
Abbeville,	9,156	28,642	12,973	54,939	$25,261
Anderson,	5,626	18,499	10,387	36,381	15,210
Barnwell,	5,715	28,117	6,201	47,724	15,012
Beaufort,	4,933	41,710	13,751	28,521	26,860
Charleston,	4,218	30,060	11,296	17,438	30,495
Chester,	5,510	18,524	9,831	31,103	19,885
Chesterfield,	1,920	9,824	3,423	18,834	4,478
Colleton,	4,420	35,953	8,975	35,443	21,883
Darlington,	3,860	15,438	6,082	36,856	11,121
Edgefield,	9,195	36,339	15,324	62,184	30,188
Fairfield,	5,297	16,021	6,924	24,424	9,949
Georgetown,	1,350	11,200	3,500	7,840	7,150
Greenville,	3,542	11,518	6,515	26,452	8,719
Horry,	712	13,182	4,857	22,196	3,636
Kershaw,	2,643	11,494	15,984	2,004	3,041
Lancaster,	2,740	10,943	6,165	15,915	8,360
Laurens,	7,123	20,475	13,289	47,222	24,085
Lexington,	3,627	15,619	6,144	27,198	10,561
Marion,	3,252	21,909	8,352	39,837	10,104
Marlborough,	2,158	9,374	2,893	15,915	6,079
Newberry,	5,908	19,660	7,183	35,666	14,089
Orangeburg,	5,036	22,507	3,523	33,383	5,364
Pickens,	3,847	14,873	7,961	32,566	9,931
Richland,	2,954	8,878	3,022	14,709	5,206
Spartanburg,	7,844	20,498	11,104	31,251	12,749
Sumter,	5,542	32,961	8,655	47,260	25,372
Union,	5,843	17,063	7,535	32,215	14,225
Williamsburg,	1,754	17,632	3,183	29,035	7,536
York,	4,196	13,695	7,949	24,021	9,815
Total,	129,921	572,608	232,981	878,532	396,354

OF SOUTH CAROLINA ON THE 1ST OF JUNE, 1840. 153

AGRICULTURE.						
CEREAL GRAINS.					VARIOUS CROPS.	
No. of bushels of Wheat.	No. of bushels of Barley.	No. of bushels of Oats.	No. of bushels of Rye.	No. of bushels of Indian Corn.	Pounds of Wool.	Pounds of Wax.
93,104	1,093	104,606	2,495	1,135,834	15,396	198
106,105	——	69,998	1,511	698,518	16,545	——
15,889	——	16,700	4,525	670,581	7,013	——
5,810	——	40,665	3,561	786,570	38,594	1,336
50	——	120,252	521	397,151	13,735	863
46,307	10	44,561	2,385	714,581	8,408	——
5,859	——	16,038	853	198,100	3,091	525
3,763	——	29,823	390	325,825	9,462	518
13,309	5	52,477	4,026	457,193	13,750	3,000
40,295	683	120,384	3,023	1,068,521	25,310	——
22,784	123	57,125	2,136	556,055	10,398	87
550	20	13,180	50	101,975	7,000	100
37,644	——	49,259	2,682	418,940	7,286	1,346
1,720	——	126	381	81,641	4,734	1,200
4,744	——	11,525	490	160,300	4,850	——
23,910	——	26,371	——	308,832	4,800	——
186,296	515	175,436	550	829,473	14,699	——
28,849	79	24,084	757	356,827	2,286	275
4,033	——	16,416	1,353	377,041	11,289	3,478
9,276	——	22,164	1,417	275,999	3,616	21
57,350	1,129	73,185	708	635,634	10,307	——
12,490	——	12,357	577	477,011	5,680	——
48,815	25	91,539	3,440	515,215	12,684	1,432
3,465	——	63,325	965	333,796	5,436	——
58,670	——	67,615	271	722,751	10,791	300
7,125	——	54,230	1,538	681,977	14,073	——
61,661	50	63,405	1,578	757,319	7,899	——
4,460	——	5,224	——	200,312	3,390	523
64,021	235	44,148	2,555	478,833	6,648	655
968,354	3,967	1,486,208	44,738	14,722,805	299,170	15,857

AGGREGATE OF THE STATISTICS OF THE STATE

DISTRICTS.	AGRICULTURE. VARIOUS CROPS.				
	Pounds of Hops.	Bushels of Potatoes.	Tons of Hay.	Pounds of Tobacco gathered.	Pounds of Rice.
Abbeville,	26	38,699	2	1,200	500
Anderson,	—	34,575	—	3,875	
Barnwell,	—	45,952	—	—	18,000
Beaufort,	—	486,753	4,595	—	5,629,402
Charleston,	—	619,507	2,135	—	11,938,750
Chester,	9	16,252	121	—	
Chesterfield,	—	21,620	1,518	395	415
Colleton,	—	178,990	22	—	5,483,533
Darlington,	25	84,812	150	400	8,000
Edgefield,	—	62,069	4,630	—	
Fairfield,	—	20,689	—	—	
Georgetown,	—	300,000	450	—	36,360,000
Greenville,	—	18,641	—	1,500	
Horry,	—	50,676	—	4,613	79,769
Kershaw,	—	10,080	84	—	
Lancaster,	—	13,793	200	—	
Laurens,	—	30,676	—	19,825	
Lexington,	—	27,733	—	—	24,000
Marion,	15	61,530	—	1,852	67,945
Marlborough,	4	29,547	1,231	80	410
Newberry,	—	33,460	—	—	
Orangeburg,	—	74,240	—	—	510,670
Pickens,	14	32,238	—	13,613	250
Richland,	—	42,584	1,976	—	
Spartanburg,	—	2,532	100	—	
Sumter,	—	263,711	5,114	—	368,505
Union,	—	23,930	—	—	
Williamsburg,	—	60,849	1,753	224	92,512
York,	—	12,175	537	3,942	5,200
Total,	93	2,698,313	24,618	51,519	60,590,861

OF SOUTH CAROLINA ON THE 1ST OF JUNE, 1840.

\	\	\	AGRICULTURE.			
\	\	\	COTTON, SILK, WOOD, FAMILY GOODS, &C.			
Pounds of Cotton gathered.	Pounds of Silk Cocoons.	Cords of Wood sold.	Value of the products of the dairy.	Value of the products of the orchard.	Gallons of Wine made.	Value of Home-made, or Family Goods.
8,526,482	266	336	$63,874	$4,936	—	$2,1248
2,349,050	—	—	—	—	—	80,444
2,804,067	240	7,333	36,174	—	—	44,684
1,544,850	25	120,000	—	—	—	11,760
2,130,224	250	17,865	15,729	1,345	—	1,220
1,844,102	—	—	25,558	—	40	52,565
268,122	250	600	11,781	1,289	200	4,845
420,910	—	4,692	36,051	53	—	14,486
1,231,985	—	350	16,942	1000	—	28,293
7,613,125	—	3,420	24,060	290	—	124,877
8,159,450	—	—	—	—	40	16,528
14,174	—	5,000	5,500	—	—	550
137,765	—	—	25,984	6,105	—	30,554
40,780	—	344	10,442	1,025	156	13,493
14,475	40	550	8,455	—	—	8,255
2,647,676	—	—	27,977	—	—	26,370
5,910,368	—	469	40,578	18,526	—	57,600
454,191	—	250	7,559	—	—	29,031
603,496	100	450	28,698	2,123	146	35,483
2,446,088	—	87	13,650	430	26	20,078
3,105,107	20	561	20,980	—	—	28,453
878,370	38	975	17,492	1,376	—	8,833
395,253	740	—	555	953	—	50,647
1,281,989	—	835	14,466	—	—	6,172
1,595,303	—	6,480	15,417	3,560	—	76,197
2,298,712	96	140	52,081	790	35	52,145
1,612,524	—	334	21,807	181	—	41,851
515,038	15	30	15,532	50	—	17,648
866,594	—	350	20,468	8,243	—	26,393
61,710,274	2,080	171,451	577,810	52,275	643	930,703

AGGREGATE OF THE STATISTICS OF THE STATE

| DISTRICTS. | HORTICULTURE. | | | | | | COM- |
| | GARDENS. | | NURSERIES. | | | | |
	Val. of produce of market gardeners	Val. of produce of nurs'ries & florists	No. of Men employed.	Capital invested.	Number of Commercial Houses in Foreign Trade.	Number of Commission Houses.	Capital invested.
Abbeville,	—	—	—	$ —	12	—	$68,000
Anderson,							
Barnwell,	$100	—	—				
Beaufort,	7,670	—					
Charleston,	30,397	$2,000	1,057	210,960	27	34	3,563,750
Chester,							
Chesterfield,							
Colleton,							
Darlington,							
Edgefield,	—	—	—	—	2	4	26,000
Fairfield,							
Georgetown,	—	—	—	—	—	3	10,300
Greenville,							
Horry,							
Kershaw,							
Lancaster,							
Laurens,							
Lexington,							
Marion,	—	139	1	20	—	—	
Marlborough,	20	—	—	—			
Newberry,							
Orangeburg,							
Pickens,							
Richland,							
Spartanburg,							
Sumter,							
Union,							
Williamsburg,							
York,							
Total,	38,187	2,139	1,058	210,980	41	41	3,668,050

OF SOUTH CAROLINA ON THE 1ST OF JUNE, 1840.

MERCE.					PROD'TS OF FOREST.		
Retail dry goods, grocery & other stores.	Capital invested.	Lumber yards and trade.	Capital invested.	No. of men employed.	Value of Lumber produced.	Ginseng, and other productions of the forest--value.	No. of men employed.
16	$178,139	—	—	—	$500	—	2
20	54,500	—	—	—	—	—	—
38	196,450	—	—	—	30,326	—	97
35	168,000	1	$1,000	73	274,900	$2,330	266
582	3,575,100	10	75,000	684	300	—	—
22	154,300	—	—	34	—	—	—
28	202,100	—	—	45	—	—	—
10	9,700	—	—	—	47,227	6,917	133
26	127,000	—	—	18	—	—	—
39	205,500	—	—	75	—	—	—
41	78,600	—	—	—	—	—	—
34	174,775	—	—	—	—	—	—
36	104,250	—	—	—	—	—	—
6	36,963	3	—	8	29,040	—	—
29	216,000	1	24,000	10	24,000	—	—
18	60,000	—	—	—	—	—	—
28	116,209	—	—	—	7,137	—	—
13	38,800	—	—	—	78,978	—	—
12	48,450	—	—	—	2,460	—	10
17	99,600	—	—	—	—	—	—
34	95,350	—	—	42	—	—	—
18	42,100	—	—	—	16,175	—	—
16	59.600	—	—	20	8,564	—	—
15	177,300	—	—	—	17,000	—	—
39	98,700	—	—	—	—	—	—
35	66,500	—	—	—	—	—	—
25	129,750	—	—	48	—	—	—
7	38,500	—	—	—	1,077	—	—
14	96,500	—	—	—	—	—	—
1,253	6,648,736	14	$100,000	1,057	$537,684	$9,247	508

AGGREGATE OF THE STATISTICS OF THE STATE

DISTRICTS.	MANUFACTURES.						COT-
	MACHINERY.		BRICKS & LIME.				
	Value manufactured.	No. men empl'y'd	Value manufactured.	No. of men employed.	Number of Cotton Manufactories.	No. of Spindles.	Value of manufactured articles.
Abbeville,	$500	2	$350	2	—	—	—
Anderson,	—	—	—	—	1	1,308	$4,250
Barnwell,	—	—	—	—	—	—	—
Beaufort,	31,620	11	2,000	10	—	—	—
Charleston,	—	—	113,890	420	—	—	—
Chester,	—	—	1,340	9	—	—	—
Chesterfield,	—	—	—	—	—	—	—
Colleton,	—	—	7,880	22	—	—	—
Darlington,	—	—	5,500	40	1	700	19,000
Edgefield,	—	—	21,000	27	1	2,000	60,000
Fairfield,	—	—	—	—	—	—	—
Georgetown,	—	—	—	—	—	—	—
Greenville,	—	—	—	—	4	1,964	72,000
Horry,	—	—	—	—	—	—	—
Kershaw,	—	—	700	—	1	120	25,000
Lancaster,	—	—	—	—	—	—	—
Laurens,	4,100	11	2,212	92	—	—	—
Lexington,	1,000	3	—	—	1	5,000	101,250
Marion,	720	5	1,210	17	—	—	—
Marlborough,	—	—	150	—	1	2,000	16,000
Newberry,	2,000	5	1,756	9	—	—	—
Orangeburgh,	—	—	16,690	400	—	—	—
Pickens,	—	—	—	—	—	—	—
Richland,	—	—	—	—	—	—	—
Spartanburg,	—	—	5,800	12	4	2,207	42,300
Sumter,	7,871	19	11,960	216	1	1,056	19,200
Union,	3,200	5	—	—	—	—	—
Williamsburg,	4,550	66	—	—	—	—	—
York,	10,000	—	970	5	—	—	—
Total,	65,561	127	193,408	1,281	15	16355	359,000

OF SOUTH CAROLINA ON THE 1ST OF JUNE, 1840.   159

| \multicolumn{9}{c}{MANUFACTURES.} | | | | | | | | |
| TON. | | \multicolumn{7}{c}{LEATHER, TANNERIES, &C.} | | | | | | |
No.pers.empl'y'd.	Capital invested.	No. of Tanneries.	No. sides of sole leather tanned.	No. sides of upper leather tanned.	No. men empl'y'd	Capital invested.	Other manufactories leather, saddl'ries, &c	Value of manufactured articles.	Capital invested.
—	—	7	2,300	3,800	19	$11,000	12	$5,000	$2,500
45	$68,000	8	2,080	3,080	17	11,700	8	2,800	500
—	—	2	5,500	10,500	16	30,500	—	10,000	7,000
—	—	6	1,970	2,406	13	6,500	—		
—	—	3	25,020	23,020	8	9,200	4	2,000	—
								4,000	—
25	20,000	4	5,200	7,300	25	18,500	10	15,500	3,200
70	70 000	8	905	3,630	16	6,275	—		
94	52,000	7	2,700	2,650	17	11,000	8	4,200	—
50	50,000	4	1,700	3,200	43	13,000	13	13,000	6,000
							1	1,000	
—	—	10	1,589	2,854	16	7,570	21	7,444	1,703
111	100,000	3	1,150	2,150	7	10,700	—		
—	—	—	3,410	4,222	—	680	114	1,460	904
55	90,000	—					1	300	100
—	—	4	1,716	2,712	16	9,200	6	18,366	12,000
—	—	—	500	666	—	—	—	2,434	—
—	—	7	4,219	5,725	21	27,995	29	1,298	—
—	—	1	1,000	750	2	8,000	—		
95	112,450	8	1,550	2,270	16	7,900	—	1,020	—
25	55,000	5	2,304	4,119	12	10,700	11	13,650	8,305
—	—	7	2,050	3,100	13	8,670	5	5,000	3,450
—	—	—	355	392	—	1,230	—		
—	—	2	800	1,040	4	1,700	—	1,000	—
570	617,450	97	68,018	89,586	281	212,020	243	109,472	45,662

AGGREGATE OF THE STATISTICS OF THE STATE

DISTRICTS.	MANUFACTURES.						
	SOAP AND CANDLES.				DISTILLE-		
	No. of pounds of Soap.	No. of pounds of tallow candles.	No. of men employed.	Capital invested.	No. of distilleries.	Gall'ns produced.	No. men empl'y'd.
Abbeville,	—	—	—	—	14	4,325	6
Anderson,	—	—	—	—	26	15,515	13
Barnwell,	—	—	—	—	—	—	—
Beaufort,	—	—	—	—	—	—	—
Charleston,	—	—	—	—	—	—	—
Chester,	—	—	—	—	—	—	—
Chesterfield,	—	—	—	—	—	—	—
Colleton,	—	—	—	—	—	—	—
Darlington,	—	—	—	—	—	—	—
Edgefield,	36,042	11,205	—	—	—	—	—
Fairfield,	—	—	—	—	—	—	—
Georgetown,	—	—	—	—	—	—	—
Greenville,	—	—	—	—	10	3,890	—
Horry,	—	—	—	—	6	179	1
Kershaw,	4,340	1,760	—	—	—	—	—
Lancaster,	79,307	12,066	—	—	—	—	—
Laurens,	—	—	—	—	64	22,299	135
Lexington,	61,840	8,239	—	—	—	—	—
Marion,	135,950	16,294	168	$300	3	456	6
Marlborough,	215,202	900	—	—	—	—	—
Newberry,	—	—	—	—	3	985	3
Orangeburg,	—	—	—	—	—	—	—
Pickens,	—	—	—	—	49	34,555	40
Richland,	—	—	—	—	—	—	—
Spartanburg,	21,343	3,012	—	—	37	6,622	—
Sumter,	—	—	—	—	—	—	—
Union,	—	—	—	—	15	4,263	15
Williamsburg,	32,303	14,535	—	—	—	—	—
York,	—	—	—	—	24	9,199	—
Total,	586,327	68,011	168	$300	251	102,288	219

OF SOUTH CAROLINA ON THE 1ST OF JUNE, 1840.

MANUFACTURES.											
RIES.	EARTHENWARE, &C.				PRINTING AND BINDING.						
Capital invested.	No. of Potteries.	Value of manufactured articles.	No. men empl'y'd.	Capital invested.	Printing offices.	No. of Binderies.	No. of daily newspapers.	No. of weekly newspapers.	No. of semi & tri-weekly newsp'rs.	No. Periodicals.	No. men empl'y'd.
$1,650	—	—	—	—	—	—	—	—	—	—	—
788	—	—	—	—	—	—	—	—	—	—	—
—	—	—	—	—	8	5	3	3	2	4	140
—	—	—	—	—	1	1	—	2	—	—	5
—	4	$16,500	40	$11,900	2	—	—	2	—	—	9
—	—	—	—	—	1	—	—	1	—	—	2
—	—	—	—	—	2	—	—	2	—	—	5
—	—	—	—	—	1	1	—	1	—	—	3
4,570	—	—	—	—	—	—	—	—	—	—	—
110	—	—	—	—	—	—	—	—	—	—	—
200	—	—	—	—	—	—	—	—	—	—	—
4,695	—	—	—	—	—	—	—	—	—	—	—
—	1	500	1	500	—	—	—	—	—	—	—
495	2	1,800	6	500	—	—	—	—	—	—	—
1,834	—	—	—	—	—	—	—	—	—	—	—
—	1	—	—	—	—	—	—	—	—	—	—
—	—	500	2	50	1	—	—	1	—	—	—
14,342	8	$19,300	49	$12,950	16	7	3	12	2	4	164

AGGREGATE OF THE STATISTICS OF THE STATE

	MANUFACTURES.						
	PRINTING AND BINDING.	CARRIAGES AND WAGONS.			MILLS.		
DISTRICTS.	Capital invested.	Value of manufactures.	No. men empl'y'd.	Capital invested.	No. flouring mills.	Barrels of flour manufactured.	No. of grist mills.
Abbeville,	$ ——	$9,800	15	$1,705	10	4,650	42
Anderson,	——	3,105	14	2,050	13	7,770	38
Barnwell,	——	7,175	26	2,735	7	880	66
Beaufort,		——		——	——	——	13
Charleston,	120,000	79,500	54	91,300	3	3,865	19
Chester,	——	2,200	12	1,025	5	8,000	24
Chesterfield,	1,000	——		——	1	——	45
Colleton,	——	——		——	1	250	12
Darlington,	——	——		——	——	——	41
Edgefield,	5,000	11,600	29	——	——	——	80
Fairfield,	——	——		——	——	4,556	16
Georgetown,	600	——		——	——	——	6
Greenville,	4,000	16,100	36	9,600	8	1,300	65
Horry,	——	——		——	——	——	51
Kershaw,	700	2,000	20	——	8	690	34
Lancaster,	——	3,245	9	1,070	2	100	9
Laurens,	——	7,595	28	2,940	20	6,168	41
Lexington,	——	1,600	7	800	30	4,579	28
Marion,	——	3,570	11	1,227	——	——	46
Marlborough,	——	2,800	9	2,000	6	1,300	21
Newberry,	——	4,380	18	1,700	15	5,214	18
Orangeburg,	——	3,890	——	——	——	——	67
Pickens,	——	5,075	18	500	9	4,050	72
Richland,	——	1,600	3	100	——	——	19
Spartanburg,	——	5,150	12	2,700	6	——	52
Sumter,	——	5,100	20	2,070	——	——	50
Union,	——	10,420	6	2,650	5	3,000	20
Williamsburg,	——	1,260	5	200	9	441	——
York,	——	2,105	68	6,318	6	1,645	21
Total,	131,300	189,270	420	132,690	164	58,458	1,016

MANUFACTURES.

MILLS.				FURNITURE.			HOUSES.	
No. of saw mills.	Value of manufactures.	No. of men employed.	Capital invested.	Value of furniture manufactured.	No. men empl'y'd.	Capital invested.	No. of brick & stone houses built.	No. of wooden houses built.
24	$50,750	86	$66,500	$35	1	$———	—	38
29	52,650	40	53,820	—	—		—	40
75	122,320	285	180,190	30	—		—	27
11	43,300	54	34,400	—	—		—	5
21	393,000	216	563,000	10,000	207	130,000	94	53
14	49,600	38	35,195	—	—		—	8
16	———	67	30,710	—	—		—	139
13	3,650	19	30,800	—	—		—	6
27	33,800	92	42,400	—	—		1	139
52	825	178	15,000	10,350	12		—	—
8	22,780	—		—	—		—	—
2	3,500	10	5,000	—	—		—	25
42	6,500	—		2,350	5	2,000	—	4
12	58,580	68	46,815	—	—		—	24
10	3,900	20	54,000	—	—		—	—
8	3,370	6	9,650	1,000	3	250	—	—
34	31,133	66	129,225	—	—		7	55
61	22,895	—		—	—		—	12
18	43,245	83	47,725	—	—		—	348
20	20,210	50	43,250	—	—		1	207
13	50,120	29	44,700	1,870	4	550	1	24
78	64,062	312		—	—		—	38
25	20,250	70	25,700	—	—		—	8
21	25,050	70	64,200	—	—		—	—
41	———	70	35,985	1,200	3		—	4
30	35,930	125	63,135	—	—		—	41
12	22,120	19	596	—	—		—	13
9	3,973	18	18,558	—	—		5	328
15	14,165	31	28,250	1,320	6	800	—	8
746	1,201,678	2,122	1,668,804	28,155	241	133,600	111	1,594

MANUFACTURES.

DISTRICTS.	HOUSES.			ALL OTHER MANUFAC'S.	
	No. of men employed.	Value of constructing or building.	Value of all other manufactures not enumerated.	Capital invested.	Total capital invested in manufactures.
Abbeville,	50	$48,000	2,000	$1,200	$84,555
Anderson,	65	17,565	—	—	136,973
Barnwell,	32	17,325	—	550	183,475
Beaufort,	30	20,000	18,100	8,000	44,500
Charleston,	908	1,059,200	—	—	1,078,630
Chester,	25	16,000	—	—	42,720
Chesterfield,	—	26,825	—	—	40,910
Colleton,	11	8,000	—	—	30,800
Darlington,	187	125,000	—	—	84,100
Edgefield,	—	—	—	19,000	127,175
Fairfield,	—	—	—	—	—
Georgetown,	42	36,350	—	—	6,200
Greenville,	26	2,550	—	—	108,800
Horry,	7	2,580	—	—	46,815
Kershaw,	—	—	14,000	—	123,700
Lancaster,	—	—	—	—	10,970
Laurens,	137	33,400	30,416	9,948	158,256
Lexington,	11	6,000	—	—	111,508
Marion,	227	24,205	—	2,744	53,960
Marlborough,	—	14,459	438	—	135,350
Newberry,	18	5,100	—	—	90,350
Orangeburg,	53	10,500	—	—	—
Pickens,	10	5,000	—	—	60,890
Richland,	—	—	—	—	72,800
Spartanburg,	2	—	—	—	160,030
Sumter,	69	22,100	—	—	143,295
Union,	20	4,870	16,060	5,000	22,800
Williamsburg,	468	16,691	1,871	—	19,988
York.	—	5,856	—	—	37,428
Total,	2,398	1,527,576	82,885	$46,442	3,216,970

MISCELLANEOUS ITEMS,

OMITTED IN THE PRECEDING TABLES.

ABBEVILLE. *Manufactures.*—Value of hardware, cutlery, &c. manufactured, $10,000; 18 men employed. Value of hats and caps manufactured, $100; 1 person employed.

ANDERSON. *Manufactures.*—Value of hats and caps manufactured, $1,525; 6 persons employed; $115 capital invested.

BEAUFORT. *Mines.*—Domestic salt: 400 bushels produced; 1 man employed; $500 capital invested. *Manufactures.*—Value of medicinal drugs, paints, dyes, &c. manufactured, $4,100; 6 men employed; $2,100 capital invested.

CHARLESTON. *Mines.*—Domestic salt: 400 bushels produced. *Agriculture.*—30,000 lbs. sugar produced. *Commerce.*—Internal transportation: 57 men employed. Butchers, packers, &c.: 37 men employed: $110,000 capital invested. *Manufactures.*—Value of tobacco manufactured, $3,500; 7 men employed; $5,000 capital invested. Value of confectionary made, $28,083; 109 men employed; $85,500 capital invested. Value of ships and vessels built, $60,000.

CHESTER. *Agriculture.*—10 bushels buckwheat produced.

CHESTERFIELD. *Manufactures.*—Value of precious metals manufactured, $3,000; 4 men employed. Reeled, thrown, or other silk made, 16 lbs.; value of the same, $80.

COLLETON. *Products of the Forest.*—Value of skins and furs produced, $543.

DARLINGTON. *Fisheries.*—175 bbls. pickled fish; 15 men employed; $500 capital invested.

GEORGETOWN. *Mines.*—Domestic salt: 850 bushels produced; 6 men employed; $1,000 capital invested. *Manufactures.*—Value of confectionary made, $1,000; 2 men employed; $600 capital invested.

GREENVILLE. *Manufactures.*—Number of small arms made, 117; 5 men employed. Value of hats and caps manufactured, $500; 2 persons employed; $200 capital invested. Paper mills, 1; value produced, $20,000; 20 men employed; $30,000 capital invested.

HORRY. *Products of the Forest.*—705 bbls. tar, pitch, turpentine, and rosin. Value of skins and furs, $52.

LANCASTER. *Mines.*—Gold: 3 smelting houses; value produced, $26,543; 45 men employed; $30,000 capital invested. *Manufactures.*—Number of oil mills, 19.

LAURENS. *Manufactures.*—Woolen goods: 2 manufactories; value of manufactures, $1,000; 4 persons employed; $2,300 capital invested.

LEXINGTON. *Manufactures.*—50 small arms made; 2 men employed.

MARION. *Products of the Forest.*—Value of skins and furs produced, $368. *Manufactures.*—Value of hardware and cutlery manufactured, $3,465; 8 men employed.

MARLBOROUGH. *Fisheries.*—250 bbls. pickled fish; 38 men employed; $1,117 capital invested. *Products of the Forest.*—10 bbls. tar, pitch, turpentine, and rosin.

NEWBERRY. *Mines.*—Granite, marble, and other stone: value produced, $1,000; 2 men employed; $500 capital invested. *Manufactures.*—Value of hats and caps made, $45; 1 person employed. Value of confectionary made, $250; 1 person employed; $100 capital invested.

PICKENS. *Agriculture.*—Buckwheat, 36 bushels. *Manufactures.*—Woolen goods: 2 persons employed; $2,090 capital invested. Value of hats and caps made, $1,580; 10 persons employed.

RICHLAND. *Commerce.*—Butchers and packers: 2 men employed; $1,809 capital invested. *Products of the Forest.*—20 bbls. tar, pitch, turpentine, and rosin.

SPARTANBURG. *Mines.*—Cast iron: 2 furnaces; 750 tons produced. Bar iron: 3 forges, bloomeries, &c.; 750 tons produced; 400 tons fuel consumed; 135 men employed in mining operations; $2,000 capital invested. Gold: value produced, $1,500; 10 men employed; $3,500 capital invested. Granite, marble, and other stone: value produced, $2,000; 2 men employed. *Manufactures.*—Mixed manufactures: value produced, $2,450; 9 persons employed.

SUMTER. *Commerce.*—Internal transportation: 68 men employed; Butchers, packers, &c.: 7 men employed, $1,100 capital invested. *Manufactures.*—30 lbs. of reeled, thrown, or other silk made; value of the same, $300; 1 male and 3 females employed; $50 capital invested,

OF SOUTH CAROLINA ON THE 1ST OF JUNE, 1840. 167

WILLIAMSBURG. *Products of the Forest.*—Value of skins and furs, $262.

YORK. *Mines.*—Cast iron: 2 furnaces; 500 tons produced. Bar iron, 6 forges, bloomeries, &c.; 460 tons produced; 5,934 tons fuel consumed; 113 men employed in mining operations; $111,300 capital invested. *Agriculture.*—26 bushels buckwheat.

TOTAL OF THE FOREGOING.

Mines.—Cast iron: 4 furnaces: 1,250 tons produced. Bar iron: 9 forges, bloomeries, &c.; 1,165 tons produced; 6,334 tons fuel consumed; 248 men employed in mining operations; $113,300 capital invested. Gold: 5 smelting houses; value produced, $37,418; 69 men employed; $40,000 capital invested. Domestic salt: 2,250 bushels produced; 7 men employed; $1,500 capital invested. Granite, marble, and other stone: value produced, $3,000; 4 men employed; $500 capital invested.

Agriculture.—72 bushels buckwheat; 30,000 lbs. sugar.

Commerce.—Internal transportation: 125 men employed. Butchers, packers, &c.: 46 men employed; $112,900 capital invested.

Fisheries.—425 bbls. pickled fish: 53 men employed; $1,617 capital invested.

Products of the Forest.—735 bbls. tar, pitch, turpentine and rosin. Value of skins and furs produced, $1,225.

Manufactures.—Hardware and cutlery: value manufactured $13,465; 26 men employed. Small arms made, 167; 7 men employed. Precious metals: value manufactured, $3,000; 4 men employed. Wool: 3 manufactories; value of manufactured goods, $1,000; 6 persons employed; $4,300 capital invested. Silk: reeled, thrown, or other silk made, 45 lbs.; value of the same, $380; 4 persons employed; $50 capital invested. Mixed manufactures: value produced, $2,450; 9 persons employed. Tobacco: value manufactured, $3,500; 7 persons employed; $5,000 capital invested. Hats and caps: value made, $3,700; 20 persons employed; $315 capital invested. Medicinal drugs, paints, dyes, &c.: value manufactured, $4,100; 6 men employed; $2,100 capital invested. Confectionary: value made, $29,333; 112 men employed; $87,200 capital invested. Paper: 1 mill; value produced, $20,000; 30 men employed; $3,000 capital invested. Ships and vessels built: value, $60,000.

STATISTICS

OF THE

EARLY AGRICULTURE AND COMMERCE

OF

SOUTH CAROLINA.

In order to afford a better opportunity for a relative estimate of the agricultural and commercial capacities of South Carolina, at successive periods, we glean from old and official documents, the following statements:

TABLE I.

Number of Vessels loaded at the Port of Charleston, S. C., in each year from Christmas 1735, to Christmas 1748, with the amount of Tonnage, &c. and the rates of Freight and number of seamen for the three last of those years.

Between Christmas	Vessels.	Between Christmas	Vessels.
1735 and 1736,	317	1740 and 1741,	246
1736 " 1737,	217	1741 " 1742,	190
1737 " 1738,	198	1742 " 1743,	206
1738 " 1739,	222	1743 " 1744,	230
1739 " 1740,	257	1744 " 1745,	208

FROM CHRISTMAS 1745, TO CHRISTMAS 1746.

No. of Vessels.	Whither Bound.	Tonnage.	Rates of Freight.	Amount of Freight.
86	Europe,	10,555	£6 10	£68,607 10
121	West Indies,	4,018	4 10	18,081 00
48	Northern Colonies,	1,720	3 10	6,020 00
255		16,293		£92,708 10

From Christmas 1746, to Christmas 1747.

No. of Vessels.	Whither Bound.	Tonnage.	Rates of Freight.	Amount of Freight.
105	Europe,	12,714	£6 10	£82,628
93	West Indies,	4,712	4 10	21,207
37	Northern Colonies,	1,332	3 10	4,662
235		18,758		£108,497

From Christmas 1747, to Christmas 1748.

No. of Vessels.	Whither Bound.	Tonnage.	Rates of Freight.	No. of Men.	Amount of Freight.
68	Europe,	8,465	£6 00	769	£50,790
87	West Indies,	4,299	4 00	499	16,196
37	Nor. Colonies,	1,189	3 00	241	3,567
192		13,953		1,509	£70,553

TABLE II.

Exports from Charleston in the year 1739.

Rice,	71,484 bbls.	Cedar boards,	3,200 feet.
Pitch,	8,095 "	Shingles,	42,600
Turpentine,	33 "	Cook stoves,	56,821
Tar,	2,734 "	Tanned leather,	1,535
Deer skins,	559 hds.	Rosin,	45 bbls.
Loose do. unpacked,	1,196	Sassafras,	4½ tons.
		Beef and pork,	539 bbls.
Indian Corn and peas,	20,165 bush.	Potatoes,	790 bush
Pine and cypress timber	209,190 feet.	SHIPS AND VESSELS. Cleared outward,	238

TABLE III.

EXPORTS OF SOUTH CAROLINA, FROM CHARLESTON, FROM 1ST NOV. 1747 TO 1ST NOV. 1748.

Rice,	55,000 bbls.	Cypr's boards,	21,000 beef
Corn,	39,308 bush.	" "	979 boards
Barley,	15 casks.	Heading,	13,975
Oranges,	296,000	"	127,652 feet.
Peas,	6,107 bush.	" pine,	148,143 " b'rds
Potatoes,	700 "	" "	1,293 boards
Onions,	10 casks.	" plank,	22 in No.
"	200 ropes.	Baywood plank,	98 "
Live stock,	28 bull'ks	Scantling,	2,000 feet.
"	150 hogs.	Shingles,	665,170 in No.
Beef,	1,764 bbls.	Staves,	132,567 "
Pork,	3,114 "	Timber,	4,000 feet.
Bacon,	2,200 lbs.	"	9 pieces
Butter,	130 casks.	Walnut,	739 feet.
Pitch,	5,521 bbls.	"	60 pieces
Tar, common,	2,784 "	Empty casks,	80 hhds.
" green,	291 "	"	43 tierces
Turpentine,	2,397 "	Hoops,	3,000 in No.
Rosin,	97 "	Canes,	800 "
Masts,	9 in No.	Pumps,	1 sett.
Bowsprits,	8 "	Beaver skins,	200 lbs.
Booms,	6 "	Calf "	141 in No.
Oars,	50 pair.	Deer, "	720 hhds.
Indigo,	134,118 lbs.	Tallow,	81 bbls.
Potashes,	3 bbls.	Lard,	26 casks.
Ol Turpentine,	7 "	"	25 jars.
"	9 jars.	Silk, raw,	8 boxes.
Cotton Wool,	7 bags.	Wax, bees,	1,000 lbs.
Sassafras,	22 tons.	" myrtle,	700 "
Boards,	61,448 feet.	Leather, tan'd,	10,356 "
Cedar boards,	8,189 "	Soap,	7 boxes.
" plank,	1,331 "	Candles,	34 "
" posts,	52 "	Bricks,	7,000 in No.

The total value of these Exports for one year:

In South Carolina currency, - - £1,129,561 06 00
In sterling money, - - - - - - 161,365 18 00

TABLE IV.

Exports of Rice for Twenty Years.

From 1720 to 1729, inclusive,—ten years, } 264,728 bbls. making 44,841 tons.

From 1730 to 1739, inclusive,—ten years. } 499,525 bbls. making 99,905 tons.

Of these Exports of the last ten years, from 1730 to 1739,

    83,379 bbls. were sent to Portugal.
       958 " " " Gibraltar.
   3,570 " " " Spain.
   9,500 " (in two years,) France.
  30,000 " " " { Great Britain, Ireland, and the British plantations.
 372,118 " " " { Holland, Hamburg, and Bremen, including about
     700 " " " Sweden and Denmark.

TABLE V.

Exports of Silk from N. and S. Carolina into Great Britain, from 1731 to 1755, inclusive.

Year.	Raw Silk.	Wrought Silk.	Year.	Raw Silk.	Wrought Silk.
1731		970 lbs.wt	1744		1,035 lbs.wt
1732		774 "	1745		544 "
1733		1,015 "	1746		929 "
1734		943 "	1747		1,313 "
1735		1,487 "	1748	52 lbs.wt	1,772 "
1736		1,223 "	1749	46 "	1,772
1737		691 "	1750	118 "	1,519 "
1738		1,111 "	1751		2,404 "
1739		1,273 "	1752		3,365 "
1740		1,454 "	1753	11 "	3,027 "
1741		2,798 "	1754		2,682 "
1742	$18\frac{1}{2}$ lbs.wt	1,576 "	1755	$5\frac{1}{2}$ "	3,416 "
1743		1,427 "			

ADDITIONS AND CORRECTIONS.

STATE OF SOUTH CAROLINA.

MORALS, MANNERS, AND RELIGION.

PAGE 18.---'The Baptists have a Theological Seminary in Edgefield,' *and another in Fairfield called the Furman Institute,* &c.

PUBLIC WORKS AND BUILDINGS.

PAGE 19.---The Santee Canal is stated to have been the first canal ever constructed in the United States.

DISTRICTS, DIVISIONS.

PAGE 28.---In the statement here made, of the districts having parochial sub-divisions, that of *Sumter* was inadvertently omitted. This district has four parishes,--- Clarendon, Clermont, Upper and Lower Salem.

On the same page,---In naming St. Thomas as one the parishes of Charleston. It should read St. Thomas and St. Dennis; the two being brought into one for political purposes.

ABBEVILLE DISTRICT.

PAGE 30.---In giving the boundaries of this district, it would be more precise to describe it as bounded on the north-west by Anderson, instead of Pendleton.

WOODVILLE, Abbeville District, formerly Greenwood, sixteen miles from the Court House, and thirty-five from Aiken, is a healthy village, pleasantly situated on a cluster of hills, and recommended highly as a summer residence. It has two Academies, one for preparing young men for college, the other for the education of young ladies. These institutions are already in possession of the suitable buildings and apparatus. The trustees have been at considerable pains to furnish a museum, and the collection is already well provided with specimens. A Lyceum has been instituted, by whose members, lectures, literary and philosophical, are statedly delivered. There is a chapel for divine worship, open to all orthodox preachers.

CHARLESTON DISTRICT.

PAGE 48.---In the sentence assigning to Charleston district its Senatorial and Representative quota, the error has been made, of giving that of the City instead of the District. Instead, therefore, of two senators and seventeen representatives, it should be ten senators and twenty-seven representatives, according to the following table, viz:

	Senators.	Representatives.
St. Philip and St. Michael,	2	17
St. John's, (Berkley,)	1	2
St. John's, (Colleton,)	1	2
St. James, (Santee,)	1	1
St. Stephen,	1	1
St. Thomas and St. Dennis,	1	1
St. Andrew,	1	1
St. James, (Goose Creek,)	1	1
Christ's Church,	1	1
	10	27

CITY OF CHARLESTON.

PAGE 53.---In enumerating the various sects of churches in Charleston, on this page, we should say, instead of 'two German,' two German Lutheran.

FAIRFIELD DISTRICT.

PAGE 77.---The Anvil Rock is described erroneously, on this page, as 'a remarkably high one.' It should read, 'a remarkable rock.' Its height is not more than fifteen feet. Its character is derived wholly from its appearance.

PAGE 78.---The population of Winnsboro is put somewhat too low, and it is fast increasing. It contains *five* and not three churches, and two or three large and elegant hotels.

GEORGETOWN DISTRICT.

PAGE.82---The trade of Georgetown, foreign and domestic, before, and for a short time after the revolution, was very considerable.

GREENVILLE DISTRICT.

PAGE 85.---The population of Greenville is underrated at 900. It is nearer 1500.

KERSHAW DISTRICT.

PAGE 88.---Kershaw is bounded on the *south east* by Sumter; *(not on the north-east;)* on the south-west by Richland, (*and not on the north-west.*)

LEXINGTON DISTRICT.

PAGE 100.---The population of the village of Lexington is underrated at 100. It should read 300.

MARLBOROUGH DISTRICT.

PAGE 104.---Here occurs another error in District boundaries which the reader will please to correct. Marlborough is bounded on the north, north-east and north-west by North Carolina; on the *south-east* (*not north-east*) *by Marion.*

QUESTIONS

ON THE

GEOGRAPHY OF SOUTH CAROLINA.

SOUTH CAROLINA.

Page	Question
9.	1. How is the state of South Carolina bounded?
—	2. State its average length and breadth?
—	3. How many square miles or acres does it contain?
—	4. Into how many classes is its soil divided?
—	5. Name them.
10.	6. Which section is famous for the growth of the finest kinds of cotton?
—	7. How is the climate in each section?
—	8. What is chiefly produced in the lower and middle sections?
—	9. What range of mountains penetrates the north-west corner of the state?
11.	10. Name the principal rivers in South Carolina.
—	11. Which unite in forming the bay and harbor of Charleston?
—	12. What peculiarity of the rivers in South Carolina distinguishes them from those of the north?
—	13. What is said of the borders of these rivers?
12.	14. What is said of the climate of South Carolina?
—	15. What was the effect of the thunder storm in the city of Charleston in 1775?
—	16. What is said of earthquakes, hurricanes and whirlwinds?
14.	17. How much of the state is supposed to be of alluvial formation?
—	18. How far does this extend?
—	19. What is said of the face of the country?
15.	20. What is the height of Table Mountain?
—	21. How many nations or tribes of Indians formerly occupied the state?
—	22. Name the chief tribes.
—	23. Name the inferior tribes.
—	24. What has become of them?
—	25. Of which tribe does a remnant still remain?
16.	26. What is their present condition?
—	27. What regions did these tribes of Indians occupy?
—	28. Give the population of the state in 1840.
—	29. Mention the number of white, free colored, and slaves.

QUESTIONS.

Page Question
16.   30. What is the military force of the state?
—   31. What is the government of South Carolina?
—   32. To whom does the right of suffrage belong?
—   33. To whom is the government of the state entrusted?
—   34. What is the number of Senators?
—   35. For how many years are they elected?
17.   36. How many members of the House of Representatives?
—   37. For how long are they elected?
—   38. In whom is the judicial power invested?
—   39. Mention the number and names of the courts?
—   40. Where are they held?
—   41. What is the metropolis of the state?
—   42. Where does it lie?
—   43. When was it founded?
—   44. What is the population of Charleston?
—   45. Which is the capital of the state?
—   46. Where does it lie?
18.   47. Where is the College of the state?
—   48. When was it established?
—   49. What is its present condition?
—   50. What is the amount of the annual appropriation to the free or public schools of the state?
—   51. What are the results of this appropriation?
—   52. What is said of the morals and manners of the Carolinians?
—   53. What is the religion of the state?
19.   54. What is said of the appropriations for internal improvements?
—   55. What is the length of the Santee canal?
—   56. What is the length of the Charleston and Hamburgh Rail Road?
20.   57. From what is the revenue of the state derived?
—   58. What are its ordinary amounts?
—   59. What is the debt of the state at this time?
—   60. By whom is the fiscal department managed?
—   61. What is the penal code?
21.   62. How many persons are employed in agriculture in the state, according to the statistics of 1840?
—   63. What is said of Agricultural Societies?
—   64. What is the influence of the State Agricultural Society?
—   65. What have been the staples of Carolina?
—   66. Which are now very little cultivated?
—   67. What have been her exports beside?
—   68. When was rice introduced, and where from?
22.   69. How many barrels were exported in 1841?
—   70. In what year was indigo introduced, and from whence?
—   71. What amount was exported at the beginning of the revolution?
—   72. In what year was cotton first cultivated in South Carolina?
—   73. How much was exported in 1795?

QUESTIONS. 179

Page Question
22. 74. How much in 1839?
— 75. Repeat what is said of the vine, the olive, and the silk-worm?
— 76. How much silk was exported in 1760?
— 77. Repeat what is said of the commerce of South Carolina?

GENERAL SUMMARY.

23. 78. When was South Carolina first discovered?
— 79. Who claimed her territory?
— 80. What was done in 1520 by Lucas Vasquez de Ayllon?
— 81. In what year did he return, and what was the result?
24. 82. Where did the colony sent out by France settle?
— 83. To what rivers did this colony give names?
— 84. What became of this colony?
— 85. What became of the second colony?
— 86. In what year did the colony of English emigrants settle at Port Royal?
— 87. To what place did they remove?
— 88. When and where did they again remove?
— 89. When did the first Indian war take place, and what was its effect?
— 90. What took place in 1682?
— 91. What in 1690?
— 92. What military expedition was undertaken in 1702?
— 93. What took place in 1703?
— 94. By whom was an attack made on Charleston in 1706.
— 95. What was the result?
25. 96. In what year was the Free School system first established?
— 97. What took place in 1712?
— 98. Who defeated the Yemassees in 1715?
— 99. When was the proprietary government thrown off?
— 100. What took place in 1728?
— 101. In what year was Charleston half destroyed by fire?
— 102. When was indigo first planted?
— 103. What took place in 1752?
— 104. When was Camden laid out?
— 105. Name the precincts into which South Carolina was divided in 1769.
— 106. What act was passed in 1774?
— 107. What took place in 1775?
— 108. What battle was fought in 1776?
— 109. Who defeated the British at Port Royal?
— 110. By whom was Charleston beleaguered, and with what success?
— 111. Who made an assault on Savannah, and what was the result?
26. 112. What battles took place in 1780?

QUESTIONS.

Page   Question
26.   113. What battles took place in 1781?
—   114. When did the British evacuate Charleston?
—   115. When was Charleston incorporated?
—   116. When was Columbia founded as the seat of government?
—   117. When was the present constitution of the state ratified?
27.   118. When was the right of primogeniture abolished?
—   119. How was the state divided in 1798?
—   120. What took place in 1800?
—   121. When was Charleston visited with a dreadful hurricane, and what was the effect of it?
—   122. In what year was the right of suffrage extended to all citizens?
—   123. When was Hamburg founded?
—   124. What events took place in 1822?
—   125. What in 1824?
—   126. In what year did the legislature pass resolutions against the protective system of the United States, as unconstitutional?
—   127. What followed in 1830?
—   128. What in 1833?
—   129. When was the State Agricultural Society established?
28.   130. Into how many districts is South Carolina divided?
—   131. Which of these is divided into two others, and for what purpose?
—   132. Name the parishes which Colleton contains.
—   133. Name those contained by Beaufort.
—   134. Those of Georgetown.
—   135. Those of Orangeburg.
—   136. Those of Sumter. (*See Appendix, p.* 173.)
29.   137. What is the number of parishes?
—   138. How many Congressional districts are there?
—   139. Name them.
—   140. Give the result of the new apportionment by the late act of Congress.

ABBEVILLE DISTRICT.

30.   141. How is Abbeville District bounded? (*See Appen., p.* 173.)
—   142. What is the soil generally?
—   143. Give the length and breadth of the district.
—   144. State the number of square acres which it contains.
—   145. Repeat what is said of its climate.
—   146. What are its principal market productions?
31.   147. What is said of its water courses?
—   148. What navigable rivers flow through the district?
—   149. What was its population in 1820, and in 1840?
—   150. How many senators and representatives is it entitled to?
—   151. Which is the chief town and seat of justice?

QUESTIONS.

Page Question
31. 152. Mention the distance of this town from Charleston, and from Columbia.
— 153. How many inhabitants does it contain?
— 154. What fortress and village in this district was conspicuous in the war of the revolution?
— 155. Where did it stand?
32. 156. Repeat what is said of this fortress?
— 157. By whom was the fort and surrounding country suddenly invaded?
— 158. What did general Pickens do?
— 159. What took place at Cambridge?
— 160. When was the first settlement in Abbeville made?
— 161. From whom is the settlement supposed to have received its name?
— 162. What religious sect is the most numerous in this district?
33. 163. What Seminary is in Abbeville district?
— 164. Name the eminent men who were natives of Abbeville.

BARNWELL DISTRICT.

34. 165. How is Barnwell District bounded?
— 166. State its length and breadth, and number of square acres.
— 167. Repeat what is said of its soil.
— 168. What are its productions?
— 169. How is the face of the country?
— 170. By what rivers is this district watered?
35. 171. By what smaller streams?
— 172. What is said of the climate?
— 173. What places of summer resort are famous?
— 174. What is the population of this district by the last census?
— 175. What is said of the increase of its population?
— 176. How many senators and representatives is it entitled to?
36. 177. Name the chief towns in this district.
— 178. Where is Barnwell village situated?
— 179. Repeat what is said of Aiken.
— 180. Repeat what is said of Blackville.
— 181. What was Barnwell district during the revolutionary war?
37. 182. Which were the most important settlements at that time?
— 183. What tribe of Indians occupied the neighborhood?
— 184. What is said of Silver Bluff?

BEAUFORT DISTRICT.

38. 185. Where is Beaufort District situated?
— 186. How is it bounded?
— 187. Name its length, breadth, and number of square acres.
— 188. What four parishes does this district comprise?

182   QUESTIONS.

Page Question
38.   189. How is the soil?
 —   190. What are the numerous islands famous for?
 —   191. Name some of the most remarkable of these upon the sea-coast.
 —   192. Name some between these and the main.
39.   193. Name the principal navigable water courses.
 —   194. What is said of the Broad?
 —   195. How is the face of this district?
 —   196. What is said of the climate?
 —   197. What has the town of Beaufort always been remarkable for?
40.   198. Name the productions of the district.
 —   199. Why is Beaufort district remarkable in the history of the state?
 —   200. What colonies settled here in 1752?
 —   201. What became of them?
 —   202. Where did the English make settlements in 1760?
 —   203. Where, and by whom, was a settlement attempted in 1762?
 —   204. What became of this colony?
 —   205. When was a permanent settlement made?
 —   206. What is the population of this district?
 —   207. To how many senators and representatives is it entitled?
 —   208. Which is the principal town in the district?
 —   209. Where is this town situated?
41.   210. What is its population?
 —   211. Which is now, and which was formerly the district town?
 —   212. What settlement was made by a Swiss colony in 1732?
 —   213. Where is Robertville?
 —   214. Where is Pocotaligo?
 —   215. What took place here in 1715?
 —   216. What British fort here was captured by the Americans?
42.   217. What eminent men were natives of this district.

CHARLESTON DISTRICT.

43.   218. How is Charleston District bounded?
 —   219. What is said of its size?
 —   220. State its dimensions.
 —   221. Name the most important islands in this district?
 —   222. Name the principal rivers.
 —   223. By what is the bay and harbor of Charleston formed?
 —   224. How far are the Cooper and Ashley rivers navigable?
 —   225. Repeat what is said of the Santee river.
44.   226. Name the inlets and bays.
 —   227. What cape is in this district?
 —   228. In what parish is Copahee sound situated?
 —   229. What is said of the soil of this district?
 —   230. What are its chief productions?

QUESTIONS. 183

Page Question
45. 231. How is the climate of Charleston district?
46. 232. Give the number and names of the parishes into which this district is divided. (*See Appendix, page* 174.)
—   233. What is the population of this district?
—   234. Which is the chief city?
—   235. What is said of the Neck?
—   236. Where is Moultrieville?
47. 237. By whom was Pineville originally settled?
—   238. What is said of Charleston city and its environs?
48. 239. By whom was the city besieged?
—   240. Mention the places in this district famous for bloody battles.
—   241. Name those conspicuous in its history.
—   242. What is its military strength?
—   243. To how many senators and representatives is this district entitled? (*See Appendix, page* 174.)

CITY OF CHARLESTON.

49. 244. By whom was it invaded in its infancy?
—   245. What is said of the situation of the city of Charleston?
50. 246. How wide is the inner harbor at its mouth?
—   247. By what fortresses is the harbor guarded?
—   248. What is the extent of the outer harbor?
—   249. How many channels for entrance to the harbor are there?
—   250. Describe these channels.
51. 251. State the latitude and longitude of Charleston.
—   252. Give the aggregate population of Charleston City and Neck.
—   253. In what year was Charleston first settled?
52. 254. When was it incorporated?
—   255. What is said of the public buildings?
53. 256. How many banks are there in Charleston?
—   357. Give the amount of their united capitals.
54. 258. What is said of the charitable institutions in the city?
56. 259. In what year was ship building commenced in Charleston?

CHESTER DISTRICT.

58. 260. How is Chester District bounded?
—   261. State its average length and breadth, and number of square acres.
—   262. Name the rivers.
—   263. Name the smaller streams which are not navigable.
—   264. What great natural curiosity is mentioned?
59. 265. When was this district first settled, and from what does it take its name?
—   266. Give the population by the last census.

QUESTIONS.

Page Question
59. 267. Which is the district town, and where situated?
60. 268. What military events took place in Chester during the revolution?

CHESTERFIELD DISTRICT.

61. 269. By whom was this district settled?
— 270. How is it bounded?
— 271. State its length, breadth, and number of square acres.
— 272. Which of the streams is navigable, and how far?
— 273. Name those not navigable.
62. 274. Give the population of the district.
— 275. Which is the seat of justice, and where does it lie?
— 276. Which is the chief town, and where situated?
— 277. What is the population of these two villages?

COLLETON DISTRICT.

63. 278. How is this district bounded?
— 279. Give its average length and breadth, and number of square acres.
— 280. Into what three parishes is it divided?
64. 281. Name the most important rivers in the district.
— 282. Name its islands.
66. 283. Give the population of the district.
— 284. In honor of whom was the district named?
— 285. How is its chief town situated?
67. 286. How did the people of Willtown distinguish themselves in 1739?
— 287. What town in this district was desolated by the Indians in 1715?
— 288. What eminent men are mentioned?
— 289. What battles were fought in this district?

DARLINGTON DISTRICT.

69. 290. By whom was this district settled?
— 291. From whom was its name probably derived?
— 292. By what river is it separated from Marlborough district?
— 293. How is it separated from Sumter and Chesterfield?
— 294. How bounded on the south-east?
— 295. Give the size of this district.
70. 296. Name the principal rivers.
— 297. Give the population of this district.
71. 298. Which is the seat of justice, and where situated?

EDGEFIELD DISTRICT.

Page Question
72. 299. By whom was this district chiefly settled?
— 300. From whence is its name supposed to have been derived?
— 301. How is it bounded?
— 302. State its length, breadth, and number of square acres.
73. 303. Which is its chief navigable stream?
— 304. Which is the next in importance?
— 305. Name the principal market towns in this district.
— 306. Give the population.
74. 307. Which are the chief towns?
— 308. How is Hamburg situated?
— 309. What is the population of Hamburg?
— 310. What village in this district is distinguished for its stone?
75. 311. By what tribe of Indians was Edgefield formerly possessed?
— 312. Name the eminent men which this district has produced.

FAIRFIELD DISTRICT.

76. 313. By whom was this district first settled?
— 314. How is it bounded?
— 315. Give its length, breadth, and number of square acres?
— 316. Name the chief rivers in this district.
77. 317. What other streams are mentioned?
— 318. Name the tributaries of Broad river.
— 319. What remarkable rock is in this district? (*See App., p.* 174.)
78. 320. What is the population of Fairfield?
— 321. Which is the seat of justice, and where situated? (*See Appendix, page* 175.)
79. 322. To what tribe of Indians did this district formerly belong?

GEORGETOWN DISTRICT.

80. 323. Where is the district of Georgetown?
— 324. How is it bounded?
— 325. State its length, breadth, and number of square acres.
— 326. Name the islands, inlets, and rivers.
81. 327. What is the population of this district?
82. 328. Which is the seat of justice for the district?
— 329. How is it situated?
— 330. What is its population?
— 331. What is its distance from Charleston, and from Columbia?
— 332. For what is LaGrange noted?
— 333. What is said of Georgetown?

GREENVILLE DISTRICT.

83. 334. Who were the original possessors of this district?
— 335. How is it bounded?
— 336. Give its length, breadth, and number of square acres.

QUESTIONS.

Page Question
84. 337. What is said of the rivers in this district?
— 338. Name the mountains within its limits.
— 339. What is its population?
85. 340. Which is the seat of justice for the district?
— 341. How is its population estimated? *(See Appendix, p.* 175.)
— 342. How far is it from Charleston, and from Columbia?

HORRY DISTRICT.

86. 343. By whom and when was this district principally settled?
— 344. From whom does it receive its name?
— 345. How is it bounded?
— 346. State its length, breadth, and number of square acres.
— 347. Name the rivers in this district.
87. 348. What is its population?
— 349. From what has its population suffered?
— 350. Which is the seat of justice for the district?

KERSHAW DISTRICT.

88. 351. By whom was the first settlement made in this district?
— 352. From whom does it take it its name?
— 353. How is it bounded? *(See Appendix, page* 175.)
— 354. State its length, breadth, and number of square acres.
89. 355. Which of its rivers are navigable?
— 356. Name the other important rivers.
— 357. Where are its most important mineral springs?
— 358. What is said of a gold mine in this district?
— 359. Give the population.
— 360. Which is the seat of justice?
— 361. How is it situated?
— 362. What military events took place in its neighborhood?
90. 363. What is its population?
— 364. What monument is to be seen in Camden?

LANCASTER DISTRICT.

91. 365. Who were the first settlers in this district, and where did they plant their colony?
— 366. How is Lancaster bounded?
— 367. State its form, length, width, and number of square acres.
— 368. What is said of the face of this district, and of its soil?
— 369. What quarries here have been worked to advantage?
— 370. Name the river which bounds the district on its longest side.
— 371. Name the creeks which may be rendered navigable.
— 372. By what other streams is the district watered?
92. 373. Mention the names of the islands in Catawba river.
— 374. What is the length of Mountain island?
— 375. How are the Great Falls of the Catawba described?
— 376. What other objects of particular interest are in the district?

QUESTIONS. 187

Page Question
92. 377. For what is Hanging Rock distinguished?
93. 378. What is said of the climate and health of this district?
— 379. What is the chief business of the people?
— 380. What is the staple production of the district?
— 381. Give the population.
— 382. What is said of the population for the last twenty years?
— 383. Which is the seat of justice, and when was it laid out?
— 384. What is its present population?
— 385. Where is it situated?
94. 386. What eminent man was born in this district?

LAURENS DISTRICT.

95. 387. By whom, and when was this district settled?
— 388. In honor of whom was it named?
— 389. How is it bounded?
— 390. State its length, breadth, and number of square acres.
— 391. What is said of its soil?
— 392. What is its principal market production?
— 393. Name the rivers and the smaller streams.
96. 394. Give the population.
— 395. Which is the seat of justice, and how situated?
— 396. What is its population?
97. 397. What is said of education in this district?
— 398. Which is the most numerous religious sect?

LEXINGTON DISTRICT.

98. 399. Where were the first settlers of this district from?
— 400. What was the original name of this district?
— 401. As a tribute to whom, was its present name given?
— 402. Where is Lexington district situated?
— 403. How is it bounded?
— 404. State its length, breadth, and number of square acres.
— 405. Where are its most valuable lands?
— 406. What are its chief products?
— 407. Name the rivers which border or pass through this district.
99. 408. Name the creeks.
— 409. Describe Ruff's mountain.
100. 410. Give the population of this district.
— 411. What is the chief occupation of the people?
— 412. What is said of the manufactures?
— 413. Repeat what is said of the climate.
— 414. Which is the seat of justice for this district?
— 415. Where is it situated?
— 416. State its population. (See *Appendix, page* 175.)
— 417. Repeat what is said of Granby.
— 418. Where is Platt's Springs, and what is said of it?
— 419. What is the character of the Academy at this place?
101. 420. Which is the most numerous religious sect in the district?

MARION DISTRICT.

Page Question
102. 421. By whom and when, was Marion District chiefly settled?
— 422. In compliment to whom was its name conferred upon it?
— 423. How is it bounded?
— 424. State its length, breadth, and number of square acres.
— 425. How is the face of this district?
— 426. Which rivers are navigable.
103. 427. State the population of this district.
— 428. What increase does this show, for ten years?
— 429. Repeat what is said of the climate and health of this district.
— 430. Which is the district town, and where situated?
— 431. What is its population?
— 432. What is the chief or only occupation of the people?
— 433. Which is the most numerous religious sect?
— 434. Repeat what is said of revolutionary conflicts in Marion.

MARLBOROUGH DISTRICT.

104. 435. By whom was Marlborough District first settled?
— 436. When was it erected into an independent judicial district?
— 437. How is it bounded? (*See Appendix, page 175.*)
— 438. State its length, breadth, and number of square acres.
— 439. How is the face of this district, and the soil?
— 440. Which is the principal river, and how far is it navigable?
105. 441. What river passes through the south-east corner of this district?
— 442. Name the streams next in importance.
— 443. Repeat what is said of the climate and health of Marlborough.
— 444. State the population.
106. 445. What is the chief market product?
— 446. Which is the market town?
— 447. Which the seat of justice, and where situated?
— 448. Which was formerly the district town, and what is said of it?
— 449. What distinguished men did this district furnish during the revolution?

NEWBERRY DISTRICT.

108. 450. By whom, and when was the settlement of Newberry District first commenced?
— 451. How is Newberry bounded?
— 452. State its average extent and number of square acres.
— 453. What minerals are found in this district?
109. 454. Repeat what is said of its soil.
— 455. What are the chief productions?
— 456. Name the two navigable rivers which bound opposite sides of this district.

QUESTIONS.   189

Page Question
109. 457. Name the two rivers next in importance.
— 458. What is said of them?
— 459. Name the other principal water courses.
110. 460. State the population of the district.
— 461. What is the chief empoyment of the people?
— 462. How is the climate?
— 463. Which is the most numerous religious sect?
— 464. Which is the district town, and where is it situated?
111. 465. How far is it from Columbia and from Charleston?
— 466. Repeat what is said of one of the curiosities of this district.

ORANGEBURG DISTRICT.

112. 467. In what year did this district receive its first white settlers?
— 468. By whom was it occupied in 1735, and by whom was this name conferred upon it?
— 469. How is it bounded?
— 470. What is its extent from south-east to north-west?
— 471. What from south-west to north-east?
— 472. What is said of the face of the country?
— 473. What of its health and climate?
113 474. How are the navigable waters of this district?
— 475. Which rivers are navigated by steamboats?
— 476. Which by small boats and lumber rafts?
— 477. What is said of Four Hole Swamp?
— 478. Name the other water courses.
114. 479. Give the population of the district.
— 480. Into what parishes is it divided?
— 481. What is the chief employment of the people?
— 482. Name the productions of the district, and the market.
— 483. Which is the seat of justice, and where is it situated?
— 484. What is said of its vicissitudes during the revolution?
115. 485. Where is Totness, and what is said of it?
— 486. For what interesting event is Fort Motte famous?
— 487. Which is the most numerous religious sect?
— 488. What eminent character, of this district, was conspicuous in the battle of Sullivan's Island?

PENDLETON DISTRICT.

116. 489. What is said of the first settlement of Pendleton District?
— 490. When was it erected into an independent judicial district?
— 491. In compliment to whom did it receive its name?
— 492. How is this district bounded?
— 493. State its length, breadth, and number of square acres.
— 494. How is the face of the country?
— 495. What is said of its soil?
117. 496 Name the rivers.
497. Give the names of the smaller streams.
— 498. What is said of the mountains of Pendleton?

Page	Question
117.	499. Name the minerals.
—	500. Describe Table Rock.
118.	501. What is said of the view from the summit of this elevation?
—	502. Name the principal objects to be seen from it.
—	503. Which is the highest mountain in South Carolina?
—	504. What is its height above the ocean?
—	505. For what is the Jocassee Valley celebrated?
119.	506. Give the population of Pendleton district?
—	507. How is this district divided, and for what?
—	508. Give the population of Pickens and of Anderson.
—	509. In what parts of the district are Pickens and Anderson?
—	510. Name the seat of justice for the judicial district of Pickens?
—	511. Where does it lie?
—	512. How far from Columbia, and from Charleston?
—	513. Which is the seat of justice for the district of Anderson?
—	514. Where is it?
—	515. How far from Columbia, and from Charleston?
—	516. Give the length, breadth, and number of square acres of Pickens.
—	517. Of Anderson.
—	518. Where is the ancient capital of the district?
120.	519. Repeat what is said of the scenery in its neigborhood.
—	520. Which is the most numerous religious sect in this district?
—	521. What is the chief occupation of the people?
—	522. Which are the principal markets?
—	523. What distinguished men has this district given the state?
—	524. What tribe of indians formerly occupied Pendleton?
121.	525. From whom did the Cherokees receive terrible defeats?
—	526. Where did Fort Prince George stand?
—	527. Where was a victory obtained over the Cherokees in 1761, and by whom?

RICHLAND DISTRICT.

122.	528. When was the first settlements made in this district?
—	529. In what year was peace made with the Cherokees?
—	530. How is Richland District bounded?
—	531. State its length, breadth, and number of square acres.
—	532. What is said of the face of the country, and of the soil?
123.	533. How is the climate?
—	534. What navigable streams bound the district?
—	535. How are the great falls of the Congaree avoided?
—	536. Name the principal of the smaller streams.
124.	537. State the population and its increase in ten years.
—	538. What is the chief employment of the people?
125.	539. Which is the principal town in this district?
—	540. Where does it lie, and how situated?
—	541. In what year was it incorporated?
—	542. What College is located in Columbia?
—	543. What appropriations are made for its support?

QUESTIONS. 191

Page Question
125. 544. What is its present number of students?
126. 545. State the number of patients in the Lunatic Asylum?
— 546. What Seminary has been planted in Columbia?
— 547. How is the town supplied with good spring water?
127. 548. Repeat what is said of the eminent men of Richland.
— 549. For what is Faust's Ford famous?

SPARTANBURG DISTRICT.

128. 550. When was the settlement of this district first begun?
— 551. How is the face of the country, and the climate?
— 552. How is Spartanburg bounded?
— 553. State its length, breadth, and number of square acres.
— 554. Repeat what is said of its soil.
129. 555. Name the rivers, and the smaller streams.
— 556. What is said of the quarries in this district?
130. 557. What ore is found in abundance?
— 558. What is said of it, and of the iron works in the district?
— 559. State the population, and its increase in ten years.
131. 560. Give the district town, and its distance from Columbia and from Charleston.
— 561. What battle fields in this district are mentioned?
— 562. How were the Americans apprised of the approach of the enemy, in the affair at the latter place?

SUMTER DISTRICT.

132. 563. In what year was Sumter first permanently settled, and by whom?
— 564. In honor of whom was it named?
— 565. How is it bounded?
— 566. State its length, breadth, and number of square acres.
— 567. How is the face of the country, and the soil?
— 568. What are the productions?
133. 569. Which rivers are navigable, and which may be made so?
— 570. What other streams water this district?
— 571. Name the lakes.
— 572. Repeat what is said of the High Hills of Santee.
134. 573. Into how many counties is Sumter District divided?
— 574. State its population.
— 575. Which is the seat of justice, and where situated?
135. 576. What is said of Fort Watson?
— 577. What eminent men has Sumpter produced?

UNION DISTRICT.

136. 578. When, and by whom was this district first settled?
— 579. What contributed greatly to increase its population?
— 580. How is it bounded?
— 581. State its length, breadth, and number of square acres.

Page Question
137. 582. Repeat what is said of Broad river.
— 583. What is said of the Tyger and Enoree?
— 584. Name the other principal streams, and the inferior ones.
138. 585. Give the population of the district.
— 586. Which is the district town, and how situated?
— 587. Of what spirited events in the revolution was this district the scene?

WILLIAMSBURG DISTRICT.

140. 588. In what year, and by whom, was this district settled?
— 589. In compliment to whom was the district named?
— 590. How is it bounded?
— 591. State its length, breadth, and number of square acres.
— 592. What is its chief market production?
— 593. What is to be seen along the edge of Santee swamp?
141. 594. Name the rivers.
— 595. Which are navigable their whole length in the district?
— 595. What is said of the Black Mingo?
— 597. State the population of this district.
— 598. Name the district town, and from what its name is derived.
152. 599. What distinguished men of the revolution has this district given birth to?
— 600. Repeat what is here said of Marion and of his operations.

YORK DISTRICT.

143. 601. In what year, and by whom, was York district first settled?
— 602. How is it bounded?
— 603. State its length, breadth, and number of square acres.
— 604. How is the soil, and the face of the country?
144. 605. What is said of the Broad and the Catawba rivers?
— 606. State the population of this district?
— 607. Which is the most numerous religious sect?
145. 608. Which is the seat of justice, and how does it stand?
— 609. Where was the chief village of the Catawba Indians?
— 610. What is said of King's Mountain?
— 611. Who defeated the British at this place?
146. 612. How many of the British were slain?
— 613. What is the height of the highest peak of King's Mountain?
— 614. Who are named of the eminent men of York District?

THE END.

www.ingramcontent.com/pod-product-compliance
Lightning Source LLC
Chambersburg PA
CBHW021148160426
43194CB00007B/729